LEGACY

a guide to
SUCCESSFULLY
TRANSFERRING WEALTH
from one generation
TO THE NEXT

LESLIE QUINSAY

DARKWOOD
—PUBLISHING—

Contact information for Darkwood Publishing
www.darkwoodpublishing.com
Email: info@darkwoodpublishing.com

ISBN: 978-1-9991773-0-0 (print)
ISBN: 978-1-9991773-1-7(ebook)
ISBN: 978-1-9991773-2-4 (audiobook)

Ordering Information:
Special discounts are available on quantity purchases by corporations, associations, and others. For details,contact: info@darkwoodpublishing.com

TABLE OF CONTENTS

Dedication

For my amazing parents, Armando & Elisa Lopez, who taught me to dream big, reach for the stars, and live my life to the fullest. I am where I am today because of your constant support and encouragement.

For my husband, Ron, who is my rock, my best friend, my business partner and fellow adventure seeker. Together we rock this world.

For my son, Ethan, an old soul filled with so much wisdom. You inspire me to give the best of myself every single day. You are the best part of my legacy.

For my brother, Junior Lopez, and my nephews Chad and Cole Lopez, who are all an integral part of our family business team.

LEGACY

a guide to

SUCCESSFULLY TRANSFERRING WEALTH

from one generation

TO THE NEXT

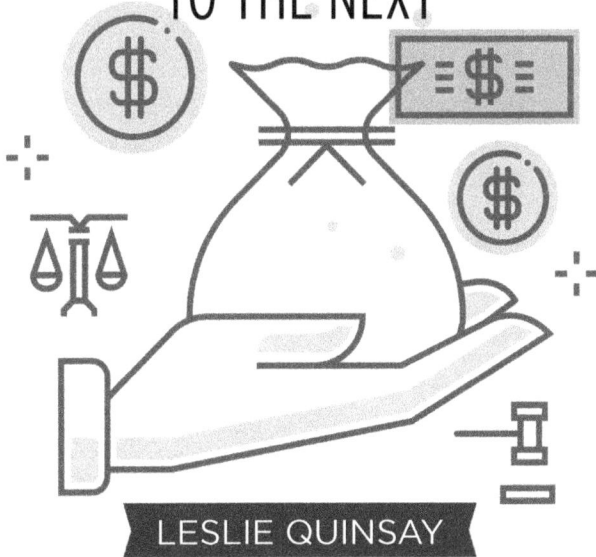

LESLIE QUINSAY

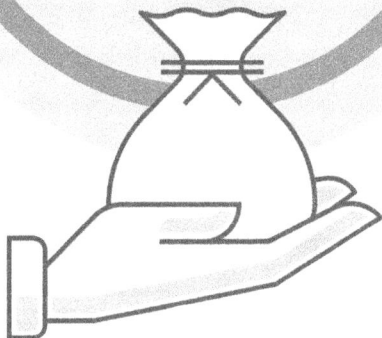

A Firsthand Emergency and No Plan

How ridiculous would it be to begin drafting an evacuation plan in the middle of a natural disaster?

Then when a fire was burning or a flood approaching, you would find yourself *planning* instead of evacuating! We've all seen the chaos that ensues when there is no plan—panic, inaction, mistakes, desperation...

We're told to plan for every eventuality—tax obligations, furthering our education, unexpected health issues, fire or theft, possible natural disasters, our vacations, and various family events—but not for our death. Imagine if tomorrow you had to take over your family's business or unravel the finances of someone who left no instructions.

"We never thought anything like that would ever happen to us." – Everyone

There are some moments in life that you remember so vividly. For me, one of those moments was an early morning dawn on a crisp winter day in December. I clearly remember being abruptly awoken from my peaceful slumber when the phone rang. A quick glance at the clock on my nightstand told me it was only 5:00 a.m. and my heartbeat quickened. Getting calls at such an early hour can only mean two things: one, some random telemarketing company has you in their system for some type of automated sales call (super annoying), or two, something bad has happened.

I jumped out of bed and grabbed the phone. "Hello?" All I remember is hearing my mom's voice telling me not to worry but to please come to the hospital.

My dad had not been feeling well for a few days, but we all thought he was just tired and sore after returning from a business trip. As it turned out, my mom had decided to call an ambulance late in the evening, worried that something really was wrong with my father. My mom is an amazing woman and her nurse's instincts proved correct. My dad was having a heart attack! Thankfully, the ambulance got him to the hospital quickly, and after having surgery to insert a stent, he was taken to the recovery room.

I remember waking up my husband, Ron, to tell him what was going on, while I threw on any clothes I could find and hurried to get on my way. I was so frazzled that I didn't even brush my teeth or wash my face, I just scrambled out the door. In my car, I called my brother and asked him to meet me at the hospital.

When I arrived, I navigated the maze of hallways to look for my mom. She had been there by herself all night because she didn't want to alarm my brother and me. That's my mom for you—always thinking about others and taking on so much herself. So, by the time we arrived, Dad was already out of surgery and in the ICU recovering. Mom took me in to see him and I have to admit I felt hesitant to go into his room. It's such a scary thing to see someone you love in a hospital bed with tubes attached and weird machines blinking and beeping.

We walked in and asked Dad how he was feeling. Although he was a bit dazed from the medication, he seemed to be doing okay. We were so lucky he had survived!

Then I shuddered to think of what would have happened with the family business if he hadn't survived!

What *would* have happened? Did Dad have insurance? Where did he keep his policy information? What about his investments, bank accounts, real estate? Did he have an up-to-date will? Who would be able to make decisions on his behalf if he became incapacitated?

After things settled down, it dawned on all of us that even though we had talked about it a little, we never really understood the impact it would have if something happened to one of us. It was as if we believed that death or health issues just didn't happen in our family. And although we had done *some* basic planning, nothing had been updated in several years.

Personal Sacrifices Had to Be Made

At the time of my dad's heart attack, I was not active in the day-to-day operations of our family business. With Dad's blessing, I was taking some time to explore my own passions, which revolved around real estate investing. But, as we sat in that hospital room and my dad became more aware of what had happened to him, he said, "You need to go to AMAG to make sure everything is okay while I recover." (AMAG is our family business and it stands for Advanced Measurement & Analysis Group Inc.)

That may not seem like much to ask, but for me it meant taking a huge detour in my life so as to attend to our family affairs. I'll talk more about that later...

Fortunately, this story has a happy ending. Although it was a long and bumpy recovery, Dad is doing fine today and is now very focused on healthy living. He reminds us all the time of how important it is to take care of our health. Without health, nothing else really matters, does it?

Our family business is also thriving. After this experience, we began to meet regularly to review where we were and to ensure that we had proper succession planning in place. We have a great team of mentors who support us, and we have spent a lot of time having deep conversations about where we all stand. We are fortunate it turned out this way, but when we stop to think about the "what ifs," we realize how unprepared we really were at the time.

As an entrepreneur and investor who works within a family business, I have seen firsthand the disastrous impact that a lack of planning can have—on one's family, staff, clients, and suppliers.

So, what is the point of sharing my story? The point is that even though we knew how important estate and succession planning were, we didn't have our act together. We were fortunate that circumstances worked out the way they did, and that Dad's health crisis didn't have a disastrous impact on our family business, but it took a life-changing emergency for us to realize the critical importance of taking more concrete steps to get our affairs in order. It's of the utmost importance to follow the advice of Stephen Covey, author of the book *The 7 Habits of Highly Effective People*. One of those habits is to "begin with the end in mind." This simple advice may seem to be just common sense, but the truth is that many of us don't cultivate that habit. *Knowing* how important something is, is not that useful if you don't *do* something about it.

Even though we had the knowledge, we didn't *take action* to put things into place until we had that scare. We had talked about it a lot but we didn't have a concrete plan regarding what to do with the family business if anything were to happen to Dad. And even if you don't have a family business, succession planning is an essential part of creating a successful, positive legacy.

I know our family isn't unique; family business enterprises are an important and vibrant part of the global economy. But there is a surprising lack of succession planning within these companies. "Succession planning is a breaking point for many family firms but only 15 percent of them have anything resembling a succession plan in place." (Source: PwC Family Business Survey 2016)

What This Book Is and Isn't Meant to Be

Before you get deeper into my book, I want to outline what this book is and isn't meant to be. It is a guide to help you work through the nuances of putting your estate and succession plan together—to give you a roadmap that can help you navigate this bumpy journey. This book addresses issues that are larger than what type of structures to set up and what documents to create; it's about legacy, emotions, impact. The goal is to get you thinking about the bigger picture —what legacy you want to leave behind and how to best communicate your intentions to your family.

Estate planning is a general concept and it applies to everyone, but it tends to get trickier when it applies to the owners of a family business. In this book I share the journey I am going through as a second-generation family business owner. I know there are many families out there going through similar issues and challenges, and I hope that this book helps to highlight some of the more informal and emotional aspects of getting your affairs in order.

The nitty gritty legal and accounting aspects of your estate and succession plan will be unique to you, and these are areas that your team of professionals will help you with. This book will help you to work through your own personal situation and to draft a plan for how you want things to be. Then it will be easier for your team to recommend structures or ways to best accomplish your big picture.

It's Not Just for Old People

It's interesting how often I hear people tell me that they haven't done any estate or succession planning because they feel it just isn't enough of a priority *yet*. It seems that many people think they are too young to have to think about it.

Personally, I have said goodbye to a number of friends and family who passed away far too young and long before they ever expected to go. The extent of estate planning that each of them had in place varied from none at all to having just a basic will. And of course, the impact, and the amount of stress that this placed on their families varied according to how much estate planning had been done, if any.

And it's not just about death. In addition to having lost friends and family members unexpectedly, I have also seen how hard it can be when accidents or prolonged illness cause strain and hardship for individuals and their families. Although you can never fully take away the challenges that arise in these situations, you can alleviate at least some of the stress by planning ahead.

Issues and Challenges

In a questionnaire I sent out to fellow entrepreneurs and business owners, I asked if they would share any estate or succession planning issues or challenges they had seen or experienced. Following is a brief list of what they shared with me.

- Unexpected illness or death is exactly that. Unexpected. When you aren't prepared and don't have adequate life insurance, planning, or strategies in place, things can be very stressful for your family, especially when you are the primary breadwinner and have dependents.

- There seemed to be fewer issues when individuals became ill or passed away in their later years. This is likely because when you reach a certain age, your family members are also older and most likely already independent.
- When family members have different relationships with money, it can cause conflict (spender versus saver, entitlement mentality versus responsibility mentality).
- When family members have invested different amounts of time caring for and helping their aging parents, it can lead to feelings of unfairness, frustration, or resentment.
- Lack of understanding of the wishes of the deceased because their will was vague or unclear.
- Stress and conflict when individuals who are assigned key responsibilities, such as trustee or executor, do not have the knowledge or skills to carry out these duties properly.
- The continuation or growth of a business becomes stagnant when the business owner becomes ill and is unable to oversee the business for a period of time.
- The decline of a business when the planned successor isn't capable of handling the executive level of work required to run the business.
- Strain placed on a business when the owner becomes injured in a serious accident and is unable to oversee operations for an uncertain amount of time and there is no other management/leadership in place.
- Disputes between family members about each person's share of a family business or their role within it.

The Great Transfer of Wealth

A study done by the consulting firm *Accenture* indicated that a great wealth transfer is underway as baby boomers age and their assets transfer to their heirs. An estimated $30 trillion dollars will transfer from this generation to the next. That's a lot of money changing hands, and the nuances of the transfer will vary from family to family. For some, the wealth transfer may skip a generation, as some baby boomers may choose to pass their wealth along to their grandchildren. Regardless of whom the wealth transfers to, those who planned ahead and organized their affairs will likely leave behind a more bountiful legacy, and there will be a more successful, and less stressful, transfer of wealth to the next generation.

In another report, Jamie Golombek, managing director of Tax and Estate Planning at the Canadian Imperial Bank of Commerce (CIBC), states, "It's surprising how many people either don't have a will or don't think they need one." He goes on to say, "If you have no will, you have no say in who will manage the estate, who will inherit your assets, or what steps could be taken to minimize taxes. Without proper planning and a written will, you are leaving it to the legislation as to who ends up with your assets, and you could be exposing your heirs to all sorts of potential problems."

I think part of the reason people hesitate to do estate planning is the word "estate." In a report written by Golombek, entitled *Your Estate Matters*, he shares common misconceptions of estate planning. According to his report, when people hear the word "estate," they may think of large sprawling properties and luxurious lifestyles. But an estate is simply *your collection of assets*. In a poll conducted by CIBC, more than half of Canadians claimed to have assets that will transfer to their heirs after their death. *On average*, the amount they plan to transfer is approximately $380,000, and that means that for many people it is much less.

No One Wants Your Junk!

Over our lifetime, we can accumulate a lot of stuff. We typically buy homes, furniture, cars, clothing, jewelry, and we may have a lot of souvenirs, knickknacks, collectibles, and personal stuff. There's nothing wrong with this, of course, but keep in mind that when it's time to go, you can't take any of this stuff with you. And although it may have had value for *you* and been meaningful to you, much of this "stuff" may not be appealing or meaningful to the people you end up leaving it to. Of course, there will often be sentimental family heirlooms but the bulk of your stuff will probably be sold or given away.

Okay, I'll admit I have a lot of stuff. For one, I have a ridiculously huge library of books. I love reading and have been collecting books all my life. I also have a few other collectibles that mean a lot to me. But if something were to happen to me today, I wouldn't be too concerned with what happens to my books or my collectibles.

What has been important to me is sharing the knowledge I learned from those books rather than passing the actual books along to my son (although some of them are rare and have a bit of value). I want to be able to pass along the wealth I have created over the years so he can continue to grow it in whatever way is most meaningful to him. Leaving him my "stuff" isn't what is important. I want to know I have structured my affairs in such a way that when I am gone, the wealth I have created is easily passed on to him.

The same goes for our businesses. Leaving behind something I have created and assuming that someone else will want it after I'm gone can lead to a messy situation. Although the business may have meant something to *me*, it may not be as meaningful to the next generation. Which means, rather than focusing on leaving my son a *business*, I want to make sure I leave behind the *wealth* that the business created. In other words, pass on the wealth rather than the business. Knowing this now allows me to structure my business and grow it in such a way that it is sellable in the event my son doesn't want to run it.

Succession Planning for Your Business

Equally as surprising as the issue of individuals not having a will are the statistics on succession planning for family businesses. A BDO Dunwoody/Compass Report on Canadian Family Business stated that "…a staggering 78% of business owners do not have a succession strategy for their business in place." The study also showed "…92% of business owners acknowledging that it was important for them to have a plan." So clearly, business owners know how important it is to put a succession plan in place, but for some reason they don't follow through with getting it done.

Additional statistics show that 87% or more of families fail to transition businesses and wealth to the *third* generation. About 65% of the transition failure is due to communication and trust issues, and an additional 20% is due to a lack of accountability and clarity. Don't let your family become one of these dreary statistics!

When you're caught up in the day-to-day running of your business, you probably don't have much time to dedicate to succession planning. This type of planning may also involve awkward or difficult conversations with family members, so business owners may choose to procrastinate and avoid the sticky web of succession planning.

Sure, you can leave it to chance and hope things just work themselves out if anything happens to you. But is it worth the risk of potentially losing everything you worked so hard to build up?

All in the Family – Life Inside a Family Business

I grew up in a very close-knit, collaborative family where the entrepreneurial spirit was an important part of our lives. From experience, I can say that a family business can be a wonderful thing, where you all work together to achieve common goals and where you all benefit from the fruits of your labor.

But it also comes with many challenges. Things can become very emotional simply because you're dealing with family. I can't even count the number of times we've sat down for a family dinner only to begin talking about work within a matter of minutes.

Love, Obligation, and Guilt

We didn't always have a family business. Both of my parents came to Canada from the Philippines and spent years working hard to provide my brother and I with the awesome lives we have today. My mom worked as a registered nurse for many years while my dad worked as an engineer in the nuclear industry.

It was only after being in the nuclear industry for over 25 years that my dad decided to retire and build a company of his own. With a Ph.D. in Nuclear Physics, my dad came at the business with a strong technical background. The learning curve for him was how to be an entrepreneur and business owner. But he decided to take a leap of faith, and he, along with several of his colleagues, formed Advanced Measurement & Analysis Group Inc., also know as AMAG.

AMAG is an engineering company that specializes in providing flow measurement equipment and measurement services to the power and process industry. Building AMAG up to what it is today was a winding and sometimes very challenging path, but our family navigated it well. I won't go into the specific details of all the ups and downs as that would be a whole other book. But I will say that having a family business taught us a lot about perseverance, dedication and focus—in order for us to achieve success. It also taught us the importance of learning to work together. My dad built this company to provide a future for us, and all of his efforts were done out of love for his family.

I never thought I'd end up working full time in our family business. Although I worked at my dad's company part time during the summers, I never saw that work as something I would pursue. After I graduated from the university, I was hell bent on becoming independent and forging my own path; the last thing I wanted was a handout. I spent the first few years after graduation working as an analyst for a mutual fund company based in Toronto. It was exhilarating at first, and I was so proud of my accomplishments. I was mostly proud that I was doing it on my own. But deep inside I felt the entrepreneurial itch.

I met my husband, Ron, during our university years and we married shortly after graduation. Ron is a proud techie nerd, and when I first introduced him to my dad, they really hit it off.

Dad eventually offered Ron a part-time job at AMAG working in the lab as part of the production staff. And within a year, he was offered a full-time position. Although working with your potential father-in-law could be intimidating, in this case it worked out well. Ron worked his way up the ranks and he now sits as the President of AMAG.

My dad never stopped asking if I wanted to work with him. It was subtle. He would ask me to participate in meetings with our accountants and lawyers—just so I would understand more about the business. But I didn't want to ride on my dad's coattails. I also didn't know if I was passionate about the business.

I eventually caved and left my job in the mutual fund industry, and I joined AMAG as the Vice President of Finance and Administration. Although I personally made the choice to come back, I think a large part of that decision was driven by a sense of guilt and obligation. After all, my parents had spent their lives caring and providing for me. How could I turn my back on helping with the business?

Then over the years, I began feeling restless. I longed to build something of my own and pursue my own passions. Although I was doing well in my role at AMAG, I didn't feel fulfilled. In the background, Ron and I were actively investing in residential and commercial real estate, and I came to realize that this was my true passion. Our real estate investment business is something we plan to continue growing over the years, and hopefully this company will transition to our son, Ethan.

I eventually told my dad that I wanted to step away from the business to follow my own dreams. And I did. I spent several years building a stronger foundation for our real estate investment business. It was amazing, and I loved what I was doing—until circumstances pulled me back into AMAG.

When Life Throws You a Curveball

Only a few short years into pursuing my real estate investment goals, Dad had his heart attack. And so, as any dutiful daughter would do, I dropped everything and returned to AMAG to take over as President. On the surface, this transition appeared seamless and effortless. But it was an emotional and trying time. I felt everything from love, obligation, and guilt to a bit of resentment. I wished we had created a proper succession plan and taken the time to talk more openly about our wants, needs, dreams, and future goals.

My dad recovered from his heart attack, and today I work with him to oversee the bigger picture. I manage the affairs of our family holding company, which owns AMAG as well as several other investments. Stepping away from the day-to-day operations of AMAG allows me to focus on creating strategies to continue to grow and eventually transition our wealth over generations. Stepping away has also allowed me time to grow my own real estate investment portfolio. Ron now runs the day-to-day activities at AMAG in his role as President.

My brother chose not to actively participate in the family business, although he does play a supporting role in graphic design and animation. And my mom plays one of the most important roles of all: She's the CEO of our family and she makes sure we don't let the business take over our lives. She provides support and encouragement, and she keeps us all in line when we get into arguments. She also forces us to stop and take time off so we can spend quality time on a family vacation every year. Although my mom and my brother don't actively work inside the business, they each have a role to play.

Over the years as AMAG grew, we began putting in place the structures that would help *transition* the wealth that we were growing as a family. We put in place a holding company and also a few intermediary companies in order to limit liability and ensure tax efficiency. Although we had the beginnings of a transition plan, there was still a lot of work to do, and this continues today as we work to update and improve what is already in place.

In this book, I have spent time sharing our family story in the hopes that if you see some parallels within your own family business, you may find many of the tips and suggestions in this book useful. Writing a book was the best way I could think of to get people thinking early on about estate and succession planning. It was a way for me to take what I have learned and experienced and leave these lessons as part of my legacy.

≡CHAPTER≡

2

CHAPTER 3

Shortsighted Thinking that Can Tear Your Family Apart

Failing to Plan Means Planning to Fail

"It was so sudden and unexpected! We hadn't really gotten around to figuring out what would happen if either of us got sick or passed away." A young mother struggles to deal with the loss of her husband who provided for their family by working as a freelance computer programmer.

"We're all so sad that he's gone, but at the same time it feels like a burden has been lifted. We've all stayed in the family business out of a sense of obligation to our parents, but the reality is that none of us are interested in continuing to run it and now we can finally entertain the idea of selling it."

"Let them deal with it. They can just split it evenly. It's easier that way," said the father. When the founder of a family business empire dies without a will, his two sons go head-to-head over control of the business. This lack of succession planning led to hurt, resentment, and conflict among siblings.

"I dedicated so many years of my life putting blood, sweat, and tears into building up a successful business, only to watch it fall apart within months." A business owner watches his business fall apart after a serious accident because there was no succession plan in place.

It doesn't matter who you are, what your background is, or where you're from. Death is the one thing the eventually finds all of us. And sometimes, even *before* death, illness, accident, or severe injury can turn our lives upside down.

Mary without Joe

Mary is a young mother with two beautiful young children. Her daughter is three years old and she has a baby boy who is 10 months old. Mary used to work as an office manager, but after she got married and had her first child, she decided that being a stay-at-home mom made more sense. Her husband Joe was the primary breadwinner and worked as a freelance computer programmer. Mary and Joe were in the prime of their life, busy with kids and activities, and they had planned a wonderful life for their family. Then Joe suddenly died from a severe heart attack. Joe was a sole proprietor, and when he died, so did his business.

Mary and Joe hadn't gotten around to doing any estate planning, nor had they put much thought into life insurance or into drafting their wills. They were young and they figured that they had their whole life ahead of them and could worry about all that stuff at a later date.

Now Mary is left unemployed, with minimal insurance, and she has two young children to raise. She will have to sell their home because she can't afford the mortgage payments (and they opted to decline the insurance protection on their mortgage). She will now have to find a job to be able to support herself and her two kids. In addition, Mary found herself in a bit of a battle with Joe's family, as he hadn't left any instructions for his funeral or burial. On top of dealing with her grief and struggling with getting their affairs in order, Mary also had to deal with that.

Bill's legacy is not what he had in mind

Bill was the proud founder and owner of a small astronomy and telescope store. His business was his pride and joy, and for over 35 years it provided well for his family. His wife worked in the business handling all of the administrative duties and paperwork, until she passed away a few years before Bill. Their three children grew up learning all about entrepreneurship from the example their parents set.

Early on, they all worked in the business—starting out with summer jobs when they were in high school and eventually each taking on key roles within the business. They all went to the university to get their respective degrees but then came back to support the business after graduating. They were good kids who saw how hard their parents worked to provide for them, and they felt that supporting the family business was their duty.

Bill was so proud to have all his children working in the business, and he dreamed of the day when perhaps the business would even pass on to his grandchildren. What he didn't realize was that his kids were working within his business out of a sense of duty and loyalty to him, but each of them had other passions and directions that they hoped to pursue one day.

It was only after Bill died, and when they began talking to one another openly about how they felt, that they realized that none of them wanted to take over nor carry on the business. It was the first time that they each felt the freedom to express their desire to exit the business, and together they decided that they wanted to sell it. They also wished that they had been able to communicate their feelings to their parents much earlier in life. They had spent years feeling trapped in the family enterprise.

Their father had seen this business as an amazing gift, built out of love, but he didn't realize that his children didn't share his passion for the business. It was indeed a gift, but it was only when he died that his children were truly able to move forward in their lives. The funds they received from the sale of the business allowed them to pursue their own entrepreneurial dreams, and they had their father to thank for that opportunity.

Dhirubhai's lack of instructions leads to bitter sibling rivalry

Dhirubhai Ambani, founder of Reliance Industries in India, passed away without a will. Upon his death, his eldest son took over as chairman of the board and his younger son became vice chairman. When the eldest brother, Mukesh, tried to boot the younger brother off the board, tension ensued and the brothers spent years fighting an ugly legal battle.

Instead of working together to build up the company, they were focused on fighting with each other. It took years and several interventions by their mother to end their feud—years that could have been spent being much more productive. If Dhirubhai had created and documented a succession plan, things could have gone much more smoothly.

John's injury and the crippled business

John was a young business owner who took over his family's store when his father retired. John's parents had run the business for almost 40 years prior to retiring. John was in his twenties when he purchased the business from his dad. He had been involved in the business all his life and he absolutely loved his work. John was single and he didn't have any children. He hadn't spent time thinking about succession planning because he felt it was too soon and not something he needed to worry about yet.

Then John got into a bad accident. He spent months in the hospital slowly recovering and unable to oversee his business. Even after coming out of the hospital, he had months of physiotherapy and was struggling with anxiety and depression. John's family and close friends stepped up and took over many of his duties while he was in the hospital. They managed to continue to operate the business, but without John there to steer the ship, some things were left unattended. As business dwindled, revenues declined, staff members had to be laid off, and slowly but surely things began to spiral downward. The business wasn't the same without John at the helm. With no instructions about what to do, who could make decisions, or who was authorized to access the company bank accounts, things went downhill. A solid business that had been around for over 40 years began falling apart in a matter of months.

Maybe you can relate to one of these stories, or maybe you haven't experienced any estate planning issues at this point. But be assured that no matter where your business is right now, one day these issues will come up. So, if you want to leave a positive legacy and not cause a lot of confusion or difficulty, it would be best to get your affairs in order.

Some of us are here for decades and others leave this world or have serious issues far too early. But regardless of when your time comes, it is important to consider what you're leaving behind. What will your legacy be?

What does my family story or any of these other stories have to do with estate and succession planning? Everything! Our story is a reminder that life is finite. We all have a limited time here. Although most of us probably don't spend much time thinking about our mortality, the truth is that you never know when your last days or day will be upon you. And succession planning is not only planning for the day we're gone, it's also planning for the unexpected accidents, illnesses, or other curve balls that life may throw our way. Preparation and planning are critical! We can choose to leave a positive, inspirational legacy by thoughtfully planning out and documenting our wishes. Or we can leave a legacy wrought with confusion, conflict, and stress. The choice is yours.

Leave a Legacy, Not a Burden

What kind of legacy would you like to leave behind? A legacy includes not only material things but also the impact you have on your family, friends, and community, whether it is important lessons, happy memories, or careful planning. If you think about your answer to the question above, it will help you to direct the way you live your life. We all have an expiry date, so make the most of your life while you are here and think about what you will leave behind.

All that being said, estate and succession planning are not always easy to deal with. They require dealing with emotions, understanding how to communicate effectively, and figuring out how to structure your affairs so that what you have worked so hard for all your life will be smoothly passed along as you have indicated.

Estate planning on its own can be fairly straightforward, but for a family business owner, it is a good idea to begin talking about and documenting a succession plan early on in order to ensure the continuity of your business (or a properly planned exit if that is your preference) in case anything happens to you. This may seem like a daunting task to a busy business owner, so to make things easier, I've created a roadmap for you to follow.

In a nutshell, your succession plan can be broken down by using the acronym "LEGACY."

L – Lay the foundation (Where are you today?) – See Chapter 3

E – Experts (Build your estate and succession planning team) – See Chapter 4

G – Goals (Incorporate your future goals into your plan) – See Chapter 5

A – Articulate your wishes (Talk it out) – See Chapter 6

C – Communication (Effective communication tips) – See Chapter 7

Y – Yield (Maximizing value) – See Chapter 8

Chapters 9 and 10 cover some of the nuances of the actual transition of wealth, and in Chapter 11, I've included a resource guide to help you get started.

≡CHAPTER≡

Lay the Foundation – Your State of Affairs Today

"Planning is bringing the future into the present so that you can do something about it now."

– Alan Lakein

I had an amazing friend named Abby who was the sweetest, kindest person in the world. She was a wife, a mother of three young boys, and an inspiration to so many of us. Abby was in her early thirties and she had her whole life ahead of her. She was working to provide an amazing life for her young family and striving to achieve the goals that were important to her. Until she got sick. It started with a few visits and short stays at the hospital. Then she was hospitalized. Then it wasn't long before my young, energetic, vibrant, and beautiful friend passed away.

It was an absolutely heart-wrenching time for her family and friends, and saying goodbye was so difficult. She was a strong matriarch who had done so much for her young family. When she passed away, her husband was left to look after the three young boys and be the single income earner.

Did she expect to die so young? No. Before she got sick, I remember her vividly sharing her entrepreneurial hopes and dreams with me. She had her whole life ahead of her and was focused on building up something great for herself and her family. Even though we all know that illness, accidents, and other misfortunes happen all the time, we somehow feel we are immune to them. But you never know when something could happen, which is why you should start early and be organized so if disaster strikes, your family will be okay.

What does your estate look like today? If you are a business owner, what would a snapshot of your business look like right now? Now would be a good time to do a review and ask yourself these questions.

Clearly understanding your position today and knowing where you plan to be in several years' time, and also beyond, will be key information that your estate and succession planning team will need to know.

An *estate plan* covers the transition of all of your wealth and should provide clear instructions on how you want things handled when you pass away. It should also cover instructions for how you want to be cared for and who can make decisions on your behalf should you become disabled or unable to manage your own affairs. If you have young children, you should provide instructions as to who will care for them and manage their inheritance until they are old enough to do so themselves. Really, an estate plan is an instruction manual for your family. For business owners, an estate plan will also include a *succession plan,* which covers the transition of the leadership and ownership of your business.

If you care about your family, you should have an estate plan and a succession plan in place, and this should be updated regularly. This is something you need to do TODAY. It's something you need to do FOR YOUR LOVED ONES.

Many people assume that in the absence of a will, their assets will simply pass to their spouse or family and their family will sort it out. This may be the case for jointly held assets and the right of survivorship. But if you die without a will in Canada, you are considered to have died "intestate." This means that the government gets to decide how your assets are distributed.

In Canada, each province has rules that dictate who your estate's beneficiaries are and how much they are to receive. I don't know about you, but I sure as heck would rather take control over who gets my stuff rather than letting the government meddle with my assets.

8 Reasons to Get Started Today
Why get started today?
- To force you to get organized and take stock of where you are.
- To provide a sense of security and stability for your family.
- To make sure your assets are distributed according to your wishes.

- To ensure continuity and/or the successful transition of your business.
- To ensure proper tax planning so as to make sure you maximize what goes to your family.
- To avoid confusion with regards to your care if you become ill or incapacitated.
- To provide instructions and financial resources for your dependents.
- You don't know when illness or death may strike.

Getting Started – What Does Your Planning Look Like Right Now?

Let's keep it simple and start with where you are today. Do you already have an estate and succession plan in place? Do you have a current will that is part of this estate plan? If so, have you reviewed it recently to make sure it is up to date based on your current situation? An estate plan is always a work in progress and should be reviewed and updated on a regular basis. If you don't have one in place, don't fret. The good news is that by picking up this book you are taking steps in the right direction to get your affairs in order.

There are many areas to consider when putting together your estate plan, so let's break it down and you can begin thinking about how you want each of these areas handled.

Your Finances – Assets & Liabilities – What's at Risk?

Understanding your net worth position will show you what's at stake if anything were to happen to you today. Large chunks of what you worked so hard to build up could be at risk if you don't put in place measures to make sure the bulk of it goes to your family and not the tax man! There's an old adage that says, "Failing to plan is planning to fail" and this is very true in the case of estate and succession planning.

Let's begin by taking a look at your finances. Creating or updating your net worth statement is a great starting point and provides a snapshot of where you stand at a given point in time.

I've included a very simple template below to help you get started. You may have many other assets and liabilities to include, such as other banking accounts, vehicles, jewellery, and other valuables, so please create a net worth statement that creates a *complete* picture of all that you *own* and all that you *owe*. Below is a very simplified example:

CURRENT NET WORTH STATEMENT			
Assets		**Liabilities**	
Principal Residence	$1,350,000	Mortgage	
Investment Property	$450,000s	Mortgage	$210,000
RRSP account	$200,000s	Line of credit	$30,000
Savings	$20,000	Credit Cards	$10,000
Total Assets	$2,020,000	**Total Liabilities**	$750,000
Net Worth	$1,270,000		

I find it useful to have a separate sheet that contains details for each of the items on your net worth statement. For instance, for your principal residence you may want to include the address, date purchased, purchase price, who is on title, name of insurance company, and policy number. For the mortgage on that property, you may want to include who the lender is, mortgage account number, payment amounts and frequency, and any other relevant information that would be important if someone had to manage this property for you.

Once you have an up-to-date net worth statement, you can begin thinking about what you want to happen to these things when you're gone. For instance, who are the beneficiaries on your accounts? What would happen to your family home? Would it pass to your spouse? And in the event that you and your spouse pass away at the same time, are there instructions for who would inherit it?

Begin getting your thoughts together so when you meet with your estate planning team, you can tell them how you want things handled. Your advisors will provide guidance on the best way to set things up, but at the end of the day they rely on you to convey to them how *you* want your estate handled.

A Succession Plan for Your Business

For business owners, theoretically your asset list would include the value of your business or shares in a business that you have part ownership of. You need to think about who you want your ownership or shares to go to in the event of your death.

If you are in a partnership, you should also talk this over with your business partner so that he or she is aware of what may transpire should anything happen to you. It's important for them to know who would be taking over for you, as this would be their new partner. If you are in a corporation, think about the impact that the transfer of your shares would have on your fellow shareholders.

In addition to the transfer of ownership, all entrepreneurs and business owners need to spend time thinking about who would take over leadership of the business. Having several exit strategies is useful and it will allow you to be prepared for changing circumstances.

If you have a family business, it's important to get a feel for whether the next generation is interested in carrying on the business. Have you had discussions about this yet? If not, now is a good time to start talking about it. If the next generation isn't interested in carrying on your business, begin building a management team (so that the business is not dependent on just you). In addition, it will be essential to identify, groom, and position the next person who will take over for you. In order to ensure successful implementation, these things must be done years in advance of any change. Again, this highlights the importance of proper succession planning.

Insurance Policies

When my husband and I got married, one of the first things we did was purchase term life insurance. We wanted to ensure that if something happened to one of us, the other would be financially okay. We were both working and had great jobs but we knew managing all of our bills and payments was dependent on *both* of us having a steady income. In an emergency or if anything happened to either one of us, the other could be saddled with a difficult financial burden.

When our son was born, this became even more important. Having someone who is dependent on you is a huge responsibility, and it's important to make sure you leave instructions and financial support for their care.

If you already have insurance in place, this is a good time to review what you have and determine if you need to make any changes. If you don't have insurance, look into the insurance options that work best for you.

Many employers offer some life and disability insurance as part of their benefits package, so take the time to understand what you may already have in place.

It's also vitally important to *document* what policies you have in place so it will be easy for your family to submit the appropriate claims and paperwork if something happens to you. My insurance agent told me stories of families not realizing that their loved one who passed away had policies in place with her office, and so there was a long delay before the families accessed the funds.

Guardianship of Minors

What arrangements do you have in place for your kids if something happens to you? If you are married, the other parent would typically continue to care for them, but they would need to have financial resources in place. Even more important is having a plan in place if you and your spouse were to die at the same time. Deciding who could be responsible for raising and supporting your kids is a huge decision. And is there such a person available?

Finding a guardian who is capable and fiscally responsible, and who would pass on your values and raise your kids the way you would like them to, is a huge challenge. Once you decide who this might be, have a serious talk with them to find out if this is a role they would be willing to take on.

Instructions For Your Care in the Event of Illness

Part of your estate planning should include instructions for how you want things handled should you become gravely ill and incapable of managing your affairs. This would include not only naming those who would have authority over your affairs but also proper legal documentation empowering them to take action on your behalf. As a business owner, think about who would be able to make decisions, sign important documents, access financial accounts, etc., in your absence.

You will also need to outline how you want to be cared for, how it will be paid for, and any specific directions or preferences.

Once you determine your thoughts on these issues, your estate planning lawyer can prepare the proper legal documentation to support your wishes.

Instructions and Arrangements in the Event of Your Death

These days it has become popular to preplan and prepay for your funeral service and burial or cremation. Funeral homes have many different options and packages you can choose from. Planning this while you are in good health and able to think things through clearly is important. Also, paying for it in advance takes the financial burden off your family.

I have a family member who has done this, and I went with her to the funeral home to work through everything. It was a strange and rather morbid experience, but prearranging everything is a great idea.

Funeral homes have different packages, options, and payment plans that you can choose from. The first step is to meet with a funeral director who will talk to you about plans, pricing, and your final wishes. It is a bit of a weird feeling listening to someone plan out the minute details of their funeral and burial. You can discuss everything from deciding your final resting spot to selecting which flowers, songs, prayer cards, and other things you want to have at your funeral. You may also be directed to a showroom filled with caskets—who knew there were so many different styles, colors, and features?

At the end of the day, the benefit of doing this is that it takes the burden off of your family having to arrange, select, and pay for things after you pass. They will have peace of mind knowing that everything has been arranged exactly the way you want it.

Baseline for Your Family Business

Just as you have put together a baseline for your *estate*, you also need to put together a baseline for your *business*. Are your financial statements and tax filings up to date? If not, get things up to date and begin reviewing your business status.

What does your organizational chart look like? Take the time to go through who is working in the business, what are their roles, and what is the chain of command. If something were to happen to you today, how would this organizational chart be affected?

Do you have other family members in leadership roles within your business? If not, is this something you are planning for? In the interim, who has signing authority for your business if something happens to you?

At this point, I'm just suggesting that you document how things stand today. Once you have a clear picture, you can begin to fill in the gaps.

Use your baseline as the foundation for your estate plan

Now that you have taken the time to think about how you want these different areas to be handled, the next step is to use this baseline to begin documenting your estate plan. This is also a good time to begin talking to your family about these issues and getting their input so you can all be on the same page.

As a starting point, I find it useful to put together your own set of draft notes on how you want everything handled. As you go through the process, you will undoubtedly have many questions. Take the time to make a list of these questions so when you sit down with your estate planning team you can review them and get clear answers on the best way to proceed.

My family and I set aside time at least once a year to meet and review where things stand and to determine if anything needs to be updated or changed. We don't always get everything done, but what's most important is that we are in constant communication with one another. My parents' and my brother's estate planning affect mine, so we have to work together on the succession plan for our family businesses.

Intergenerational Family Planning

I am part of what has been called the "sandwich generation," which means I am juggling the needs of my aging parents while raising a young family. At this particular stage in life, it's important to begin tying together your and your family's estate plans. In our case, we also own an intergenerational family business, so part of our planning includes passing on a legacy and not just a business.

Over the last few years, I have been meeting with my parents and brother more often to determine what my parents' needs will be over the coming years. It's important for my brother and I to work with them to ensure their plans are up to date and reflect their wishes.

Our conversations revolve around things such as what type of care they want as they get older, where they will want to live, and how we can best support their wishes. We also talk about the wealth they have built over the years so we can understand how they want things handled. Part of their planning includes things they want to set up or structure for my son and my nephews.

My husband and I also plan for our own family unit. On top of working in the family business, we have our own company, which primarily invests in real estate and real estate related projects. We have also begun to have conversations with our teenage son about his plans for the future, and we educate him on what we have in place so he will have a head start. We also emphasize that we want him to follow his own path and that he shouldn't feel obligated to carry on anything we have created if that is not where his interest lies. As Tom Deans emphasizes in his book, *Every Family's Business*, it's important to focus on transitioning the *wealth* and not necessarily the *family business*.

We want our son to know he is free to build his life around what he is passionate about. This is why early communication is so important. For example, if he has no intention of taking over our investment company, we must be prepared with multiple exit options. Knowing this in advance, and taking the time to ensure that our business is built so it will be sellable down the road, is very important. Talking about it openly and early also alleviates any pressure that my son might feel when it comes to our family business.

As Ethan gets older and begins earning an income and acquiring assets, we will talk to him about estate planning for his own future.

Be Proactive versus Reactive: A Succession Planning Lesson

A few years ago, I attended an executive development program at Harvard University. It was a program aimed at educating business owners on how to best lead their company through its life cycle. During my week-long stay, I met many fellow entrepreneurs who shared similar issues and challenges. As I began writing this book, I was reminded of one of the younger guys in our group. He was at the course to network and to leverage the knowledge and experiences of the other entrepreneurs.

During one of our case study sessions, we explored the impact of death or illness on a business. The case study we reviewed was about an established business owner who suddenly had a stroke and could not run his business for several months. His family was not involved in the business, and he didn't have a plan in place. His business suffered and almost fell apart while he struggled to recover.

The story reminded me of my dad's sudden heart attack and the impact it had on our family, so I shared our story with the class. As I recounted what happened to our family, I saw a young man making eye contact with me and nodding emphatically. Soon after, others nodded and raised their hands to share similar stories.

During our networking break, the young gentleman that I just mentioned came over to talk to me. He hadn't shared his story during class, but he came over to ask me more questions about how I was managing things. He opened up and told me that his family owned a real estate development company in Europe, and he shared that his father had experienced a fatal heart attack. Due to the lack of proper planning and transitioning over the years, this young man felt stressed out, overwhelmed, and somewhat resentful about being thrown into his family business so unexpectedly.

If they had openly discussed and planned for what would happen to the family business in the event of an emergency, things would have been much smoother. It's never easy to deal with illness or loss, but if you include estate and succession planning as an integral part of your life, your family will be in a better position. Do it for *them*.

It's a Work in Progress

Once you are clear on your baseline, you can begin communicating with your family and sharing your thoughts with your advisors—typically an estate planning lawyer and possibly your family accountant. This will allow you to document and create your estate plan based on your current situation. Remember that an estate plan is more than just a will. It involves proactively planning the transition of your assets to your family members. Typically, an updated will comes out of this process, along with a game plan for how to structure, hold, and manage your assets over the years.

Keep in mind that estate planning is an ongoing process. Your life situation and position will be constantly changing over time, and it's important to modify and update your estate plan as this happens.

Minding the Gap - Estate and Succession Planning that Covers Your Future Plans

Now that you have read about the consequences of not planning for unexpected future events, I hope it brings home the idea that although where you are today is a great starting point, effective estate planning should cover the gap between where you are today and where you hope to be a few years down the road. We will discuss your future goals in Chapter 5.

Now that we've covered reviewing and documenting your current situation, I suggest building the team that will help you get things in good order. Begin working with your advisors to share with them a solid picture of where you are today. From there, you can begin having conversations that will include your goals for the future, so you can get a better understanding of the steps you should take to ensure your estate and succession planning will line up with your goals and plans.

≡CHAPTER≡

Experts – Who Should You Draft for Your Team?

By now you've hopefully begun to discuss things with your family and together you have come up with an idea of how you might handle your affairs. Hopefully, you have all survived and are still speaking with one another. And if not, no worries; your job has just become easier as you can go ahead and cut the annoying individuals out of your will. Of course, I'm totally joking, and there will still be a lot to discuss and review with your family; but at this point, it's a good idea to begin thinking about the professional team you will need to support you in the process. They will guide you, provide options and strategies, and put together all the necessary documentation to make everything legal and binding. With the informal baseline you have put together, you can begin to build your team and lean on them to help you complete the process.

Estate and Succession Planning Is a Team Sport

It's important to build a solid team that will work with you to create, document, and execute your estate and succession plan. When creating your team, make sure the people you choose to work with are a good fit for you and for your family. This is a sensitive topic, so you have to be comfortable sharing information and talking openly with your team. You may need to interview multiple consultants until you find the ones that you think are best suited for you.

Just as with any venture or sport, you will need people on your team that have different areas of expertise. Who should be the key players on your team?

The Estate & Succession Planning Consultant – Your Guide

As I suggested previously, I highly recommend finding an experienced and reputable estate and succession planning consultant, especially if you have a complex situation. A great consultant will take the time to meet with you and all your family members who are involved and will listen carefully to all of your concerns and issues. They should ask questions to understand how things are structured and what you already have in place.

Once they have had an initial consultation with all of you, they will typically set up sessions to meet with each family unit individually. For example, our consultant sits with just my parents to make sure they can get proper advice without being influenced or pressured by us. My brother and his family have their own session, and my husband and I and our family have our own session. Each of our families has different nuances and concerns, and a good consultant will understand how these things may interact. For example, being prepared for unexpected life circumstances like separation or divorce is important. Even though no one ever plans for these things to happen, the reality is that they do. If these things do happen be sure to update your estate and succession planning documents to reflect your new life circumstances.

Once you have had your initial meetings with your estate and succession planning specialist, you can start to involve other professionals to provide advice and guidance so that you are covered in all areas. This is discussed below.

Attorney (one who specializes in estate and succession planning)

You'll need a lawyer who focuses on estate and succession planning. If you don't already have a lawyer you work with, your specialist/consultant should have a database of professionals they can refer you to. Make sure you are comfortable with whomever it is you choose to work with.

Your estate and succession planning lawyer will typically be focused on things from a liability perspective. Lawyers are trained to think about worst case scenarios, so they will create structures that will protect you and your assets and will ensure that they are passed along in a manner that works best for your family's situation.

In addition to illness or death, they may address how to best set things up in the event of other major life changes such as divorce, getting remarried, children, stepchildren, the best way to set up a new business partnership or corporation, and other such issues. Basically, a good lawyer will work to set things up to *minimize* your risks and liabilities.

Chartered Accountant

You need an accountant who will work closely with your lawyer and your estate and succession planning consultant to make sure any planning you do is tax efficient. They will look at what you already have in place and recommend the best way to structure things so as to accommodate your estate and succession plans. Also, when you share your future plans, they can help you make sure that what you are putting in place has room for the growth you are anticipating.

Make sure the accountant you choose has a solid understanding of the tax implications and regulations around estate planning. If you already have someone to help you with your personal and business affairs, that's great. If they work for a larger firm, they can also recommend people or resources within their organization to support you.

For instance, the accountants we use have been working with our family for many years, and they know our personal and business situations. In addition, when we began adding US real estate to our portfolio, they were able to bring in one of their associates who specializes in that area so as to make sure we were doing things right.

Tax Implications

When you die, the executor you appointed will have to file a final tax return. Upon death, you are deemed to have disposed of all your belongings. As when you are alive, when you dispose of assets and you have made money, you have to pay tax. When it comes to your estate, you should ask your accountant to talk to you about how to best structure things in order to reduce taxes.

Assets are often passed to a surviving spouse tax free. The disposition of these assets will then be taxed upon the death of the surviving spouse. If you plan to leave some of your assets to someone other than your spouse, be sure to ask what the tax liability and impact will be on the person receiving the inheritance.

Probate Fees

In Canada, in addition to paying taxes on property disposed of at death, many provinces also impose a probate fee. This is a fee that is charged for the process of having a will approved by the courts and confirming the appointment of an executor. Probate fees are usually a percentage of the value of the estate and can add up to a hefty amount. Work with your accountant to see if there are ways to do things in order to reduce the amount that will go through probate. For instance, designating beneficiaries for your registered funds will ensure that those funds go directly to the beneficiary and will not be included in your estate when calculating probate fees. Other things you can consider are joint ownership or giving things away early on.

Estate Freeze

If you are a small business owner, you can ask your accountant if it may be beneficial to do an *estate freeze*. This transfers the future growth of a business, investment, or asset to other family members.

As I keep repeating, each individual or family has specific circumstances unique to them, so there is not one best way to do things. Having an accountant who understands your unique situation will ensure that they can help put together a plan that is best for you and your family.

Financial Planner

Some of you may have financial planners who oversee the bulk of your portfolio. If you feel comfortable including them, it may make it easier for them to provide quality advice for you. They may not need to be involved in all stages of the process, but if they understand what your lawyers and accountants are putting in place, they can make sure that they manage your portfolio in a way that will tie into your long-term plans.

Insurance Agent

It's important to talk to an insurance specialist to make sure you have adequate coverage. Again, your insurance agent may not need to be involved in all stages of your estate and succession planning, but it is a good idea to review what insurance you have and determine if you need to make any changes or purchase additional coverage.

If you have a young family who would need support if anything happened to you, then you should have an insurance policy in place, one that provides them with enough so they won't have to struggle. Over time, your family may not be as dependent so you can always reduce the amount of your insurance coverage.

The two main types of life insurance are *term* insurance and *whole life* insurance. A term policy is one that covers you for a set period of time—usually 10, 15, 20, or 30 years. A whole life policy is permanent coverage that lasts a lifetime and has guaranteed premiums and a guaranteed cash value.

You need to review your own situation and consider what type of life insurance is best for you. What type of coverage do you have in place, or do you need, for your investments, businesses, etc.? What about your other family members? Do their insurance policies need to be revised or updated?

Don't forget to include any disability or insurance policies you may have from your workplace. For instance, the group benefits package at our company includes some disability and life insurance. If your family isn't aware of this and something happens to you, it may take awhile before they realize it, and this will delay submission of a claim and the subsequent payout.

In addition, this would be a good time to review your beneficiaries and update them if there have been changes in your life or in theirs. Once everything has been reviewed and updated, it's a good idea to have the details of all of your policies, along with contact information, in one location (preferably with your estate and succession planning documents). This way it will be easy for your family to find and submit whatever claims are necessary.

Leading Your Team

Take charge! You are the leader

Once you have a professional team in place, it is important that they work together effectively. Each one brings a different area of expertise to the table, and their efforts will need to be coordinated so they are not stepping on each other's toes. You are the leader of this group, so it is up to you to be clear about your goals—what you hope to accomplish and what your expectations are from each of these professionals.

Gather your team for periodic meetings

Although you can meet with any of your team members separately, I think it is useful to have a few meetings where you bring everyone together so they're all on the same page. I know how challenging it can be when I'm trying to explain to my accountant some of the strategies my lawyer has suggested, or vice versa. In the end, I often have them call one another because that's the only way to make sure that the communication is clear and that there will be no misunderstandings.

Don't be afraid to ask lots of questions

Another important tip is to make sure you and your family *understand* what they are recommending. I realize all the legal and accounting mumbo jumbo can be a bit confusing and complicated, but there's no sense in setting something up if you don't understand its purpose or how it works. Ask lots of questions, and if in doubt, get independent advice from another professional.

My family and I have been in situations where we're sitting in a meeting with our lawyers and accountants and it feels like they're speaking another language. Often, they can get caught up in debating complex structures and suggestions, and they forget that we may not have a full understanding of what they are talking about. Yes, we rely on them to give us solid advice, but *we* have to be accountable for making the final decisions. So, seriously, if you don't understand what they are saying, or understand what they are suggesting, keep asking for clarification until it makes sense to you. Don't worry about looking silly or feeling stupid. It's your life and your assets on the line, so do what you need to do to protect your family's interests.

Clearly Communicate Your Objectives

When I first began writing this book, one of the first things my writing coach asked me was, "What are your goals with this book?" Only by taking the time to understand exactly what I was trying to accomplish was my coach able to guide me along a path that would take me to where I needed to go.

If *your* objectives aren't clear, it can be hard for your team to structure and devise an effective plan for you. The end result will only be what you had hoped for if you are clear and concise upfront. This is why a lot of the hard work of soul searching and talking things out with your family happens *before* you get to this phase.

This goes back to the concept of *beginning with the end in mind.* If you are clear on what you want the end result to look like, it will be much easier for your team to help you get there. You may find that once you start clearly outlining what you want, your team may have other suggestions for you to consider. And it's okay to tell them you need *time* to think about and review these alternative solutions before you decide how you want to proceed.

Timelines

When it comes to estate planning, the best time to do it was *yesterday,* but the next best time is *now.* Regardless of where you are in life, at least get things in order based on your current situation. Going forward, you can review this on a regular basis and make updates as your life circumstances change. Typically, doing a brief review once a year will be sufficient.

With regards to succession planning for your business, the time is also *now.* Take inventory of where you are and map out where you plan to be in the next few years. As we discussed, you will have to start putting things in place *today* if you want to achieve the milestones you have set for yourself.

In terms of exit strategies for your business, you need to begin planning your exit several years before your planned exit date. So, for example, if you're in your mid forties and you want to retire by the age of 50, you need to start building your exit team *now*.

Also, once you get started, don't let anyone rush you if you reach a point where things aren't making sense to you or if you are having trouble understanding what your professionals are recommending. This is where it is okay to stop and take the time to thoroughly think things over and to make sure you are happy with the direction in which they are taking you. As I stated before, *you* are the leader, so you can always choose to slow down the process and ask for clarification.

Teamwork Makes the Dream Work

As with many things in life, great things are possible when a group of people come together to achieve something. Estate planning is not something you should try to tackle alone. Surround yourself with individuals who are strong in the areas in which you need support and guidance. You will be amazed at what can be accomplished if you let others help you along the way.

≡CHAPTER≡

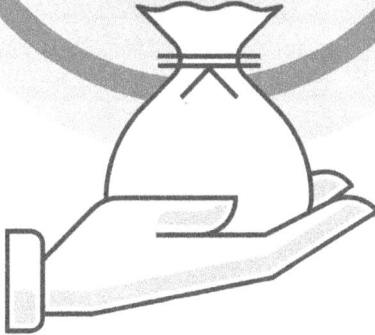

Goals — Hindsight Is 20/20 so Let's Begin at the End!

Carve your name on hearts, not tombstones. A legacy is etched into the minds of others and the stories they share about you.
    – Shannon L. Alder

One of my favorite movies of all time is *A Christmas Carol* by Charles Dickens. My family used to gather at my parents' house every Christmas Eve, and I remember sitting in front of the TV to watch it while waiting for our guests to arrive. As the Christmas tree lights twinkled and the smells of roast turkey, potatoes, and vegetables filled the house, I would sit and watch as Ebenezer Scrooge, a cranky old businessman, is visited by the ghost of his dead business partner, Jacob Marley. Jacob wants to show Scrooge that if he continues on his current path, the legacy he will leave behind will not be a meaningful one.

Unlike Scrooge, most of us will never get the opportunity to take a sneak peek into our future, but with proper estate and succession planning we can take control of the legacy we leave behind when we die. Doing so requires having a clear picture of where we are today and of what we're working toward over the coming years.

How much time do you spend thinking about and planning your future? If you're like the majority of people, you probably spend the bulk of your time hustling every day to pay your bills, grow your wealth, grow your businesses, and acquire more. You're doing this while juggling your day-to-day responsibilities, caring for your kids and sometimes your aging parents, and all the other things that come with being a grownup. It's all part of this whirlwind thing called life.

Beginning with the end in mind means that we focus on the following things:

- Impact
- Pursuit and achievement of goals and dreams
- Beyond you—passing things on to the next generation

Impact

What is your purpose in life? What do you hope to achieve before you die? After you are gone, what will happen to everything you have built up? What stories will people tell about you? What memories and lessons have you left with your family and friends?

To be effective regarding your estate and succession planning, it's helpful to think about the mark you want to leave on the world after you are gone. By understanding the impact that you want to have, you can begin structuring your affairs so as to ensure that you will accomplish what you envision.

To get a clear picture of how things will be after you are gone, let's fast forward through time and take a look at what your funeral will look like. The first thing you will probably see is your grieving family. Are they struggling to make funeral arrangements because they are uncertain as to what you may have wanted? Are they fighting over how to go about things? Are they able to carry the financial burden of paying for your funeral? Are they clear on the things that need to be taken care of now that you are gone?

By looking forward in time to this emotional moment, you can begin to see that with careful preplanning and communication, much of the stress of planning a funeral can be alleviated. This may be something you want to consider as you begin your estate plan. Maybe you are able to afford to pre-arrange and prepay for your funeral today. If not, maybe that's something you want to begin saving for so the burden is not left with your family.

Looking forward at this moment will also force you to think about what financial protection you have in place for your family. If you have a business, making sure that you have a succession plan in place for leadership and ownership will be extremely helpful for your family, especially if they are not active in the business themselves. Businesses often fall apart because the founder becomes ill or dies. This can be prevented by thinking about the future of your business now.

Another thing to think about might be: What memories and lessons have you left behind? This is the intangible stuff. What might your eulogy sound like? Do you like what you hear, or do you need to make changes today to ensure that the impact you leave behind is what you hoped for?

A good way to help shift your mindset toward what your long-term goals are, is to think about what you would like your eulogy to sound like. What would your spouse or partner have to say? How about your children? And how about your friends, mentors, business associates, and colleagues?

Steve Jobs is the well-known—but often misunderstood—cofounder, chief executive, and chairman of Apple Computers. After he passed away in 2011, the New York Times published "A Sister's Eulogy for Steve Jobs." It was a touching and heartfelt piece written by his sister, Mona Simpson, and it shared the impact that he had on her life and a few of the key things that she learned from him. She wrote about how he was in his various roles as a brother, husband, father, and businessman. Steve Jobs accomplished much more in his 56 years than many people ever will in a full lifetime. His focus, determination, and perseverance, even while sick, allowed him to reach the goals and dreams he had set for himself.

The eulogy captured the essence of Steve Jobs' life throughout its different phases. But what is obvious is that without having a clear, compelling vision to keep him on track, none of it would have been possible. He was focused and driven because he had a strong purpose and a solid foundation. Even amidst all the obstacles and challenges, he was steadfast in pursuing and achieving his goals.

At the time of his death, Jobs had an estimated net worth of over $7 billion, and at the time people wondered what would happen to the fortune he had amassed in his rather short life. Even though we will never know the extent of Steve Jobs' estate planning, it appears that he did things right. An article in Forbes in October 2011 discussed the implications for Job's fortune had he not done the proper planning. In addition to a hefty estate tax bill, he also had a complicated family dynamic with children from different relationships. It would have been important for him to outline exactly what was to be left for each of his children in order to prevent conflict. It is believed that Steve Jobs protected his estate with living trusts, among other things. This helped to keep his affairs private and it minimized estate taxes. Because of his careful planning, not only did he leave behind memories and lessons by the example he set, he also ensured a financial legacy for his family.

I'm not saying we should all aspire to be like Steve Jobs, but I do believe that to live a productive and fulfilling life, we each need to have our own solid vision and goals to work toward. There must be a purpose in all that we are doing. And one of the most important things to remember is to include estate and succession planning as part of the process. As you reflect on how you want to be remembered, it may make it easier to figure out your purpose, your vision, and the plan that will allow your efforts to be passed from generation to generation.

One day we will die and we can't take our stuff with us. So, in setting our vision and goals, we should consider how to successfully pass on our wisdom, memories, and wealth to the next generation.

Goals & Vision - What does your finish line look like? - Structuring your estate and succession plan to accommodate your future goals and dreams

"The loftier the building, the deeper the foundation must be laid."
– Thomas A. Kempis

Picture yourself sitting atop the Burj Khalifa at the dizzying height of 828 meters. That is one extremely tall building and it requires a lot of support to keep it stable and steady. Building the foundation for this majestic structure required over 45,000 cubic meters of concrete, which weighed over 110,000 tons! It also features 192 piles that are buried more than 50 meters deep. As you can imagine, erecting this building would not have been possible without first investing the time, materials, and manpower to build an extremely solid foundation to support it.

Goals work in much the same way. The bigger your goals are, the deeper your foundation will need to be. Even though the foundation isn't visible after a structure is built, we all know that it is there beneath the surface, holding everything up and ensuring that what is built will stand the test of time and all that nature hurls at it.

Estate and succession planning are a crucial part of this foundation! When it comes to goals, it works the same way, but instead of concrete, rebar, and piles, the foundation for your goals is your purpose, attitude, skills, mentors, support team, financial resources, and your estate plan. Your purpose and attitude hold you steady when obstacles and challenges appear. Your skills, mentors, and support team serve as the engineers that make sure you have the correct structures in place. And your financial resources ensure that you can afford to invest in the things necessary to achieve your goals. But it's your estate plan that ensures that all you have built up will withstand the test of time by being thoughtfully and carefully passed on.

You may be wondering why I'm spending so much time talking about vision, goals, and the future in a book that's supposed to be about estate and succession planning. Well, the truth is, most of you are probably not planning to die today or tomorrow. Most of us may still have years or decades of life left to live.

So, when working on your estate and succession planning, what is most important is what your estate will look like at some time in the future. Of course, it's still important to have your affairs in order in the event of your unexpected demise. But I think what would be most worthwhile would be to begin structuring your affairs so they accommodate your future plans.

Here's an example. One of the pillars of wealth in my family is real estate. My husband and I own several rental properties that we started acquiring when we got married. We had a simple goal of purchasing one property per year and we didn't have a child when we first got started. Based on our situation at the time, the easiest and best option for us was to hold these properties jointly in our personal names. If something happened to one of us, then full ownership of the property would go to the surviving spouse.

Even before purchasing our first property, we spent many months build-ing up our foundation. We read everything we could about investing, spoke with our family members and friends who were already investing, signed up for courses and seminars, and began talking to realtors, lawyers, accountants, and property managers. We wanted to make an educated in-vestment and also to ensure that we were surrounded by a team of people that could support us in achieving our goals.

We bought our very first property in Milton, Ontario—a new, sin-gle-family townhome. So, much work went into getting to the moment when our lawyer handed us the keys. And once our property manager took over and got it rented, we were on cloud nine—having accomplished this milestone that we had set for ourselves. When some of our friends found out that we had purchased another property, they commented on how lucky we were to have been able to do this. But it had nothing to do with luck. They didn't see all the background work that went into building the foundation. All they saw was the end result. The reality was that the actions we took toward building our solid foundation were what allowed us to achieve success.

Over time, our portfolio grew, and it expanded from being primarily single family residential to including larger commercial properties. We also got involved with other real estate related investments, such as first and second mortgages, joint ventures, and limited partnerships. On the family front, we were blessed with a wonderful son a few years into our marriage. Before we had a child, our affairs were structured so that if something hap-pened to one of us, everything would go to the other. Pretty simple, right?

As our life situation changed and our real estate goals expanded, we re-alized (thanks to the advice of our amazing legal and accounting advisors) that there might be a better way to structure how we held our properties. We also included plans for how our wealth would transition to our son after we were both gone. We had to improve and reinforce the original foundation we had built in order to support this growth.

We formed a corporation for some of our real estate investments and began acquiring new properties within this structure. As we continue to grow our portfolio, we meet with our advisors regularly to ensure we are doing things in the best way possible. This new structure helps reduce our liability, is more tax efficient, and allows for the smooth transition of these properties to our son one day.

Once we had a child, we suddenly had to think about who would care for him, support him, and guide him through life if anything happened to us. Whereas life insurance didn't seem like such a big deal earlier on, we now realized how important it was so our son would have financial resources if anything happened to us before he was fully independent. Our structure is a work in progress and we continually work with our advisors to improve or modify how we do things.

The accounting and legal details behind our changes were based on our personal situation. Each individual situation is unique, so although this is a path that works for us, it may be different for you. Don't make the mistake many others do and just copy what someone else is doing. Your accounting and legal advisors will be able to walk you through options that are best suited for your current situation and your plans for future growth. This isn't a legal and accounting book but rather a resource guide to help you navigate the turbulent and emotional waters of estate planning.

If your long-term goal is to eventually pass your business on to your children and have them run it, then it's important to talk to them now to make sure this is something they are willing to take on. In your mind, you may believe that you are leaving them an amazing gift. But if it's not what they want, you are really leaving them a huge burden. Understanding this and talking about it at an early stage will allow you to modify your estate and succession plans if need be.

Let's hit the fast-forward button and see what your life looks like 10 years from now

Where do you expect yourself to be 10 years from now? Are you single or married? Or maybe divorced? Are you still actively managing your business? Are you traveling more? What does your net worth statement look like? What will your investments look like? Are you drawing upon your retirement savings or still actively building it up? Are your children interested in working within your business? Do you even know where you want to be in 10 years time? Are your current actions bringing you closer to getting there?

It's okay if you don't have all the answers yet. Many of us haven't spent much time thinking about the details of where we expect to be down the road. That may be part of why you picked up this book. So, let's shift to thinking about your ideal future life using some goal setting exercises and tools. If you already do these things, that's great! You can probably go straight to the next section. But if this is new to you, now is a good time to get started. There are many ways to do this, but I'll share three concepts that I have found particularly powerful.

1. Create a vision board.

I've been using vision boards for many years and I find them to be a creative and fun way to document my goals. The concept is simple; it involves gathering images that reflect the goals you are working toward and using them to create a visual display. There are no rules regarding the format or what to include, so feel free to showcase your goals in your own unique way. Be creative and have fun with it!

You can use a bulletin board, a collage picture frame, a Bristol board, a photo album, or an electronic version. I do recommend creating something that you can hang up on the wall and look at every day, as it's powerful to see your goals right there in front of you. Feel free to include things like a net worth statement, quotes you relate to, or phrases you find inspiring.

2. Write a detailed description of your ideal life 10 years from now.

Write a few paragraphs about your ideal life 10 years from now. Write it in the present tense, as if you have already accomplished the goals you set for yourself. The more descriptive you can be, the more helpful this exercise will be. Be thorough in describing how it feels to have accomplished all these things and even include sensory details of what you see, hear, smell, feel.

Here's a sample prompt to illustrate how to get started:

Today is (insert a date 10 years from today) and I am sitting on my front porch watching the sky turn different shades of yellow and orange as the sun rises. The birds are chirping and I feel the crisp morning air on my face, as the aroma of my morning coffee awakens my senses. I am enjoying this morning ritual knowing that I am now financially free and that my investments are creating enough income to support my lifestyle.

3. Family/friend wealth creation meetings.

Find or develop a group of people with whom you feel comfortable sharing your goals. Sharing your goals will help keep you on track and accountable. As author Shawn Achor discusses in his book, Big Potential, you can achieve much more when you develop, contribute to, and tap into a network of people who lift you up. It's important to surround yourself with a group of supportive and like-minded individuals who will listen to your goals without judgement. My family does quarterly wealth creation meetings where we take time to share our goals and dreams with one another and we serve as accountability partners. We also challenge and push each other to continually raise the bar. Having regular meetings is our way to stay focused and energized. If you are an investor or business owner, you can also find or create a group of fellow investors or business owners to do this with.

These are just a few ways to begin focusing on and documenting your goals, and there are many other methods. The most important thing is to take action. Also, keep in mind that you can use these methods to create goals for all aspects of your life, whether they be financial, health and wellness, personal improvement, or spiritual. For the purposes of this book, I've primarily used business and financial examples.

You may have heard of the SMART acronym for goal setting. Whether you use one of the above exercises or your own variation, I suggest you format your goals so they meet all of the SMART criteria.

Specific – Be very clear in describing what you are trying to achieve.

Measurable – Make sure each goal can be measured. If not, it will be hard to track your progress along the way, and it will be difficult to determine whether or not you have successfully achieved that goal.

Attainable – Are the goals you have set within reach? Are they achievable?

Realistic – How practical are the goals you are aiming for?

Timely – Make sure your goals are time-bound. Set a specific target deadline for achieving each goal.

When you set your goals, remember to include an element of estate planning.

A Roadmap to Achieving Your Goals

Now that you've thought about and documented your personal, financial, and business goals, let's take some time to create a basic roadmap to help get you there. It's motivating and exciting to have something to look forward to, but without a plan to help you get there, it's all just pie in the sky. You may wonder why we're addressing this in a book about estate and succession planning, but remember that in order to put the best plan and structures in place, you need two key pieces of information: 1) where you are today, and 2) where you are going. By identifying where you are going, it will be easier to include estate and succession planning tools and strategies that will tie into your big picture.

In his book, *The 7 Habits of Highly Effective People,* Stephen Covey talks about beginning with the end in mind. He encourages his readers to use their imagination to envision their goals. His philosophy stems from the understanding that all creation begins in the mind, so in essence everything is created twice: Once in our mind as an idea and then a second time in the physical world. We've used this approach to help you focus on and create your goals. Now we'll use it again to help you figure out exactly what you need to be doing today in order to reach your future targets.

Create a 10-5-3-1-Year Plan

At this point, you're probably thinking, "Great. So, I've jotted down some big goals I'd like to achieve, but how am I ever going to get there?" The truth is you won't always know the "how to" upfront.

An effective method for breaking a larger goal down into manageable chunks is to create a 10-5-3-1-year plan. Take those long-term goals and work backwards to determine what needs to happen today in order to achieve your goals. This is really your best guess at where you need to be each step of the way in order to hit your target. By setting milestones, you give yourself a basic roadmap to follow.

As a business owner, I've often used this tool with my team. When brainstorming and creating a vision, we must then take the time to think about what needs to happen at each step along the way in order to make our vision a reality.

For instance, let's say we have clients only in Canada, but our 10-year goal is to become internationally recognized and have clients in five other countries. Maybe by year five we need to have sales in three or more countries. Maybe by year three, we need to have sales in at least two new countries. Maybe by year one, we need to have at least one international sale.

This isn't an exact science but looking at the big picture in this way will help you to establish specific goals.

Linking Your 10-5-3-1-Year Personal and Business Goals to Your Estate and Succession Plan

From an estate and succession plan point of view, we have to work backwards to understand what we need to put in place today to ensure continuity. For instance, if you plan to retire in 10 years, who will run the business? If it's one of your children, that may mean that by the five-year mark they are active in a management position. Working backwards further, it may mean that in year three you involve them in the business planning activities.

Let's say your goal is to pay off your mortgage in 10 years or less. Work backwards to figure out how much you need to pay down the principal each year in order to achieve this. In the end, you need to determine what works for you, as this plan is designed specifically for you. Ten people may share this same goal, but we can expect that there will be 10 different pathways to get there. What's important is that you work backwards to set up milestones and then track your progress along the way.

When it comes to your investments and possessions, you can also use the 10-5-3-1 plan to ensure things fall into place. Using the example above, you can project what you think your property may be worth at the 10-year mark. Perhaps you plan to downsize in 10 years. This might mean that in year five you talk about doing renovations and improvements to your home so it is in a good position to be put on the market. From an estate and succession planning point of view, you may decide to buy your "downsized" home in cash and then invest extra funds to create a stream of income when you retire. Or perhaps you want to set up a trust fund for your grandchildren. There are many different directions you can choose, and your estate planning team can suggest strategies to help you achieve your goals.

John Doe's Sample Plan - January 1, 2019

Here's a sample plan to illustrate the process. Feel free to use one of your own goals as we go through this exercise. Within each section, there will be estate or succession planning issues to address or plan for.

10-Year Goals (These are the BIG goals, the ones you have on your vision board, etc.)

My home will be fully paid off by September 30, 2028.

I will have a net worth of $5 million on or before December 31, 2028.

I will own eight investment properties by December 31, 2028.

I will sell my business for $10 million or more by December 31, 2028 (succession plan milestone).

5-Year Goals

I will have a net worth of $3 million on or before December 31, 2023.

I will own seven investment properties.

My business will be valued at $6 million or more by December 31, 2023.

I will have an advisory board in place by December 31, 2023.

I will have an exit team in place by November 30, 2023 to help me prepare for the sale of my business.

I will hire a chief operating officer to oversee my business by September 31, 2023.

3-Year Goal

I will have a net worth of $2 million on or before December 31, 2021.

I will own four investment properties.

My business will be valued at $3 million or more by December 31, 2021.

My business will have two or more international clients by December 31, 2021.

1-Year Goal

I will have a net worth of $1.5 million on or before December 31, 2019.

I will own two investment properties.

My business will be valued at $1 million or more by December 31, 2019.

I will hire an International Business Development manager on or before December 31, 2019.

To show how I worked through the net worth component of my plan, I've included a sample spreadsheet I used to create my projections for net worth. It may look complicated but it can be simplified to suit your needs. At this point, you don't need to have all the details down to a tee. I just happen to love spreadsheets, so this is my way of creating a plan to achieve my goals. This spreadsheet also includes the *assumptions* I made.

I took the written goals above and mapped out what needs to happen each year to accomplish my big 10-year goals.

Sample Spreadsheet - Net worth projections

Don't get too caught up in the minute details of the plan. Just view this as a way to keep yourself on track. It's also a tool that allows you to see where you could be each step of the way, which is important for your estate and succession planning. As you begin to hit your milestones, be sure to update your estate and succession planning documents to reflect the changes in your life.

Are you leaving behind a wonderful legacy or a messy burden?

Now that you've thought about your long-term goals and developed the milestones, let's get back to estate and succession planning. Assuming you achieve your goals, let's take a look at what you will leave behind when you're gone.

Most people leave a family home, some savings or investments, and a bunch of personal belongings. Some will have monetary value and some are more of sentimental value. If a person has a will in place, it may be fairly straightforward.

ASSUMPTIONS
Properties appreciate 3.5% per year.
My principal residence mortgage will be completely paid off in 10 years.
Residential investment properties will be purchased with a 25 percent down payment and 25-year amortization periods.
Multi-unit/commercial property mortgages will be purchased with 40 percent down and 20-year amortization periods
Will purchase one additional real estate investment property by end of year one.
Will purchase two additional real estate investment properties before end of year three.
Will purchase three additional multi-unit properties before end of year five.
Will purchase one commercial real estate investment property by end of year 10.
Will add $10,000 to RRSP each year.

END OF YEAR 10				
Assets			**Liabilities**	
Principal Residence	$ 1,904,308		Mortgage	$ -
Investment Property 1	$634,769		Mortgage	$144,665
Investment Property 2	$551,973		Mortgage	$220,060
Investment Property 3	$502,550		Mortgage	$234,765
Investment Property 4	$564,151		Mortgage	$229,257
Investment Property 5	$564,151		Mortgage	$229,257
Investment Property 6	$593,843		Mortgage	$241,323
Investment Property 7	$593,843		Mortgage	$241,323
Investment Property 8	$975,000		Mortgage	$585,000
RRSP account	$300,000		Line of Credit	$ -
Savings	$35,000		Credit Cards	$ -
Total Assets	$7,128,295		**Total Liabilities**	$2,119,092
Net Worth	$5,009,203			

END OF YEAR 5				
Assets			**Liabilities**	
Principal Residence	$ 1,603,377		Mortgage	$269,188
Investment Property 1	$534,459		Mortgage	$179,840
Investment Property 2	$464,747		Mortgage	$269,395
Investment Property 3	$423,134		Mortgage	$280,012
Investment Property 4	$423,134		Mortgage	$280,012
Investment Property 5	$475,000		Mortgage	$285,000
Investment Property 6	$475,000		Mortgage	$285,000
Investment Property 7	$500,000		Mortgage	$300,000
RRSP account	$250,000		Line of Credit	$15,000
Savings	$25,000		Credit Cards	$ -
Total Assets	$5,173,850		**Total Liabilities**	$2,163,447
Net Worth	$3,010,403			

END OF YEAR 3				
Assets			**Liabilities**	
Principal Residence	$ 1,496,769		Mortgage	$365,793
Investment Property 1	$498,923		Mortgage	$192,463
Investment Property 2	$433,846		Mortgage	$287,101
Investment Property 3	$395,000		Mortgage	$296,250
Investment Property 4	$395,000		Mortgage	$296,250
RRSP account	$230,000		Line of Credit	$25,000
Savings	$20,000		Credit Cards	$6,000
Total Assets	$3,469,538		**Total Liabilities**	$1,468,857
Net Worth	$2,000,681			

END OF YEAR 1				
Assets			**Liabilities**	
Principal Residence	$ 1,397,250		Mortgage	$456,633
Investment Property 1	$465,750		Mortgage	$204,333
Investment Property 2	$405,500		Mortgage	$303,750
RRSP account	$210,000		Line of Credit	$25,000
Savings	$20,000		Credit Cards	$8,000
Total Assets	$2,498,000		**Total Liabilities**	$997,716
Net Worth	$1,500,284			

CURRENT NET WORTH STATEMENT				
Assets			**Liabilities**	
Principal Residence	$ 1,350,000		Mortgage	$500,000
Investment Property 1	$450,750		Mortgage	$210,000
RRSP account	$200,000		Line of Credit	$30,000
Savings	$20,000		Credit Cards	$10,000
Total Assets	$2,020,000		**Total Liabilities**	$750,000
Net Worth	$1,270,000			

In addition to the physical assets you leave behind, you may also have some life insurance to help ensure surviving family members are taken care of.

As an entrepreneur or investor, however, your situation may be more complicated. You may leave an operational business behind, a large portfolio of properties, and/or other investments. You may have complex structures you were advised to set up or a tangle of corporations that must be managed. What happens to these things when you're gone? Who will be responsible for taking over your business? Are your family members already involved in the day-to-day operations of your business or will it be difficult for them to manage? Do they understand how everything is structured and what their role is?

In these instances, it's extremely important to have exit strategies in place. I suggest that you begin to think about, and write down, the current state of things today and what would happen if you were no longer here tomorrow.

≡CHAPTER≡

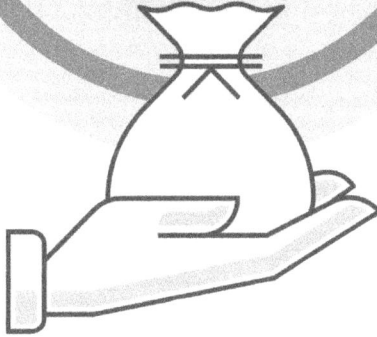

Articulate Your Wishes –
Don't Let Family Ties Turn into Family Feuds

"Sticks and stones may break my bones, but names will never hurt me." Hmmm, maybe so, but when it comes to estate and succession planning, fighting within your family can be more hurtful than any physical pain.

There's nothing more gut wrenching than watching family members get into huge fights and disagreements when a loved one passes away or becomes ill. Especially when they're fighting because they didn't know how things were to be handled or how assets were to be distributed. Or, in some cases, when a family member expects something will pass to them and they find out they weren't included, intentionally or not.

You need to clearly articulate your wishes so that when the time comes, there won't be any confusion. This part of the communication is about *you* and how you want things to be. It's about being clear in stating your wishes.

In the next chapter, we will cover the other side of things—namely, how others receive your message, and how to best communicate with them, given that we all receive messages differently.

Leona Helmsley was a famous American businesswoman who was known for having a mean streak. She truly earned her nickname as the "Queen of Mean" when she left more to her pet dog, Trouble, than she did to her grandchildren. She did leave something for two of her grandchildren, but the other two received nothing at all. The two who received nothing brought the issue to court, and in the end, the judge determined that Leona was mentally unfit while drafting her will. Trouble's inheritance dropped from $12 million to $2 million, but that was more than enough for her beloved pet to live a luxurious life. (CBS News, article by Sean Alfano on August 29, 2007 – "Leona Helmsley Leaves $12M to Her Dog.")

Did she really intend to hurt two of her grandchildren? Did she really think leaving such a large amount of money to her dog was the most effective way to leave a legacy? We will never know. Maybe she had good reason for excluding them and leaving everything to Trouble; but in the end, her wishes weren't followed. In any case, make sure you take the time to state your wishes when you are still healthy and of sound mind.

Some Interesting Statistics

Bank of Montreal Wealth Management published a report in March 2017 entitled "Estate Planning for Complex Family Dynamics." The report shared the results of some of the surveys they had conducted regarding estate and succession planning. One survey showed that 40 percent of those surveyed had not had essential and open conversations about their estate intentions with their children.

In this same report, two quotes in particular highlight the importance of communication.

"Many people think you can avoid conflict by not having conversations. The truth is you can only delay conflict, not avoid it. Conflict usually escalates the longer you put off talking about things. For the least amount of conflict and the greatest level of harmony, talk early and talk often!" – Dr. Amy D'Aprix

And:

"Your children are going to read the will someday…it's crazy for them to read it for the first time after you're dead. You're not in a position to answer questions." – Warren Buffett

We Don't Know What We Don't Know

Here's another simple case that may be more relatable. I share it because it emphasizes the importance of getting your estate planning affairs in order AND communicating with your family at an early stage.

Grandma Nora passed away when she was 96 years old. Her husband had passed a few years earlier, so it was her children who made the funeral and burial arrangements. If everyone had been on the same page, things would have been easy-peasy. But there was a lot of disagreement, fighting, and emotional drama over how things would be handled. In this case, it wasn't about assets or business at all. It was about Grandma Nora's wishes for her funeral and burial…

Grandma Nora had been a practicing Catholic all her life. So, even though she didn't leave specific instructions about what type of arrangements she wanted, most of the family assumed that a Catholic funeral would be the most suitable. Had she been able to articulate this basic information while she was alive, it could have prevented a lot of family turmoil. While planning her funeral, one of her children (who practiced a different faith) mentioned that Grandma had told him on several occasions that she respected his faith and that she would like a service that would honor his faith as well. However, she never said anything about this to anyone else.

You can imagine the emotional chaos that ensued. The family was torn and they fought about what to do. In the end, the majority of her children won out and proceeded to plan a Catholic funeral and burial. Sadly, one of her children chose not to attend the service or burial because he felt disrespected, hurt, and unheard. Because of this, he missed his chance to say his final farewell, which I'm sure weighs on his mind even today. Grandma Nora would never have intentionally set up things in a way that would have her children fighting, but by not leaving clear instructions, turmoil ruled the day.

Not only did this lead to an uncomfortable feeling for everyone at Grandma Nora's service, it also meant that the ongoing communication about handling her estate was strained. Even though time will hopefully heal the hurt that this family experienced, there may be some underlying animosity between the siblings.

And this was a small and simple estate. Imagine how much worse it can be with a more complicated estate. Add more assets, business issues, and poor communication skills to the mix and you have a recipe for disaster.

When it comes to your assets, business ownership, or the legalities of who oversees the process, you can imagine the stress and confusion that can ensue if no clear instructions are left behind. Especially if your family members aren't familiar with what you have, how your assets are held, or what your business is all about. This is why *communication* is a critical part of the process. Communication can be either verbal in the form of conversations that you have while the person is still living or it can be in the form of written instructions.

What a waste of a life if you invest your heart and soul into building up something amazing, only for it to crumble and fall apart due to a simple lack of planning. And to add to this, you are hurting your family and causing them undue stress by leaving them to sort out the mess you have left behind.

So, let's move forward and take a look at what you can do today to avoid this nightmare.

It all starts by thinking of life like a relay race. You're running your leg of the race today, but at some point, you will have to pass the baton on to the next runner. In order to make this work smoothly, you need to work together long before it's time to pass that baton.

Work Together for Success

To do things right, you need support and guidance to help you achieve your goal of successfully passing the baton. This may include family members, advisors, and other professionals to motivate and guide you.

Oddly, when it comes to estate planning, we often *don't* include the people that it will most affect. Maybe it's because death seems like such a sad, solitary event and we don't want to talk about it with our family for fear of causing them stress or sadness. But by excluding them, we are harming them down the road because we are leaving them to deal with what we have left behind and there are no clear instructions.

By including your loved ones in your plans, you are allowing for a much smoother and happier transition.

Face to Face, or Facetime to Facetime

One of the things that our family does regularly is hold what we call "family wealth creation meetings." These meetings allow us to share ideas and support one another and also to set the foundation for other, more in-depth family meetings.

The main purpose of the meetings is to get together in person, share our goals and dreams, and support each other in achieving them. This includes offering each other advice, guidance, and referrals to our networks if needed. Even though the focus is on wealth creation and the achievement of goals, the conversation often does include a piece of estate and succession planning.

Having regular communication, and taking the time to better understand one another, allows us to deal with any potential areas of disagreement or stress before they become full blown and hard to manage.

When it comes to our family business, having these regular meetings allows us to express how we feel about the business and what we plan for our futures, and to make changes along the way if we are not in sync.

When it comes specifically to estate and succession planning, I find it useful to schedule dedicated time to talk to one's family and share plans with one another. In my case, this means gathering my parents, my brother and his family, and my own family to share openly how we feel about the way things are going at present. It also gives us the opportunity to talk about: a) how my parents want things handled when they are gone, b) what the future plans are for our active family business, AMAG, and c) how our family holding company will eventually transition through generations.

In addition to this, we have smaller meetings with each of our immediate families—so my parents talk amongst themselves, my brother does his planning with his family, and Ron, Ethan, and myself spend time talking about our own estate and succession planning.

Talking things out openly can be emotionally challenging, as some of the conversations can be difficult and raw. Nevertheless, this will allow for a smoother transition with minimal conflict down the road.

Here are a few tips for handling emotionally challenging conversations:
- Prepare in advance so that you can be clear about what you are trying to communicate.
- We have two ears and one mouth, so use them proportionately. In

other words, one of the most important things you can do is really listen to what others have to say.

- Don't be afraid to show your emotions. And if others get emotional, let them feel their emotions and work through them as well.
- It's okay to disagree. The point is to get your areas of concern out in the open. You might not come to a satisfactory solution right away, but you all need to agree that it's okay to disagree, and sometimes that means leaving an issue on the table for another day.
- For estate and succession planning, we use an estate and succession planning consultant and a team of lawyers, accountants, and financial planners. This ensures that we have input from the professionals who understand how the laws and systems work. We chose our team together and, when necessary, we invite them to our family meetings to help us work through certain issues.

Communicate Openly and Often

I can't emphasize enough the importance of open and tactful communication. Estate and succession planning can be a delicate subject, and emotions can run high because you are discussing a difficult topic. It can be easier to hold your feelings in rather than express them openly because you don't want to hurt anyone's feelings. But this lack of communication can lead to people making incorrect assumptions, and it can lead to resentment and hurt.

I suggest taking the time to think through your thoughts thoroughly before jumping into a conversation. If you try to express yourself in a heated moment, you will often fail to get your point across effectively.

Also, communication doesn't always have to be oral, although I find in-person meetings to be the most effective. Not only do you hear what others are saying, you also have the benefit of reading their nonverbal cues and sensing the emotion behind what is being said. Nevertheless, some may find it easier, especially in certain situations, to write a letter or email to explain their thoughts or feelings on a particular subject. Use whatever form of communication you find to be most effective for you and your family.

Having private family conversations is the first step to creating an effective and useful estate plan. Take the time to get the initial conversations underway and sort out some of the kinks, and then when you are ready you can reach out to your team to begin putting together the documents and structures needed to design your unique plan.

For families with more complicated situations, I often suggest using the services of a reputable and experienced estate and succession planning consultant who can help you dig deeper and ensure that you cover all areas that need to be addressed.

Also, communication doesn't always have to be in the form of formal, scheduled meetings. It can be as simple as a casual conversation about what your kids' plans are for the future. For example, I find that my son and I have some awesome conversations while we're in the car. We chat about day-to-day things, but from time to time I find we have some pretty deep conversations. I like hearing what Ethan is considering when it comes to his future. I also ask him about his thoughts on our family businesses and whether or not he has any interest in them. My goal is to include him in discussions early on so that as we move forward with our planning, we can be mindful of and respect the direction he may choose.

8 Tips for Effective Communication

Here are some tips that I've found useful over the years. Whether for business meetings or casual discussions, these tips help me have more productive and meaningful communication.

- Be an engaged listener. If you truly want to be a good communicator, it all starts with being a good listener. Really take the time to understand the other person's point of view. Ask questions to clarify and to show that you are truly interested in what they have to say.

- Don't interrupt when someone is talking. When you do this, the other person gets irritated; their mind remains focused on what they were trying to say, and they won't pay much attention to whatever you say.

- Think before you speak. Say what you need to say but do your best to think of how it will resonate with the person you are speaking to. Learn to be tactful when discussing difficult situations.

- Be mindful of your body language. If your body language makes you appear to be closed off (i.e., arms crossed, etc.), it may be hard for the other person to feel comfortable having a deep conversation with you.

- Manage your stress level. Communicating when you're frustrated or angry never goes well. If you feel yourself getting heated or frustrated, take a few deep breaths and calm yourself down before speaking. If necessary, it's okay to step away and let the other person know you need time to digest things or clarify your thoughts.

- Stay focused on the topic at hand. Try not to get distracted or deviate from the topic being discussed.

- Be open to feedback and diverging opinions. Although constructive criticism can be hard to swallow, be open to it and don't automatically become defensive.

- Assert yourself effectively. Communicating well doesn't mean you have to be aggressive to get a point across. Speak clearly, stay grounded in communicating the things that are important to you, and be okay with others having different opinions.

Lower Your Expectations Regarding How Things Will Be Handled

This probably sounds like a weird thing to do, but trust me, life can be so much smoother when we stop placing unrealistic expectations upon others. You can set the bar for yourself as high as you want but don't set the bar for others.

Also, thinking that everyone will be okay and will know what to do if anything were to happen to *you* is selfish. Lower your expectations and realize that people need guidance and instruction in times of sadness and grief. Sure, you may feel your spouse is awesome and fully capable of taking care of things in your absence, but if you really love your family, you'll take the time to make sure there's a plan in place.

Your Heirs May Not Care

When it comes to succession planning for businesses, many family businesses have founders who hope their business will be a legacy that carries on for generations. But you can't assume this without first talking to your children and even your grandchildren. What if no one in the family wants to carry on the business? With no plan in place for succession, a business can fall apart very quickly. You may believe or hope that your children are interested in your business and highly capable of running it, but the truth may be that they are neither interested nor particularly capable.

Lower your expectations and realize that it may be useful to have a Plan B just in case. When my dad had his heart attack several years ago, I basically dropped everything I was doing to go back into the business. But what if I hadn't had the years of experience and familiarity with the business? Or, what if I had chosen not to go back? And what if my husband hadn't been working in the business? Depending on the answers to those questions, things could have turned out very differently, and the value of the business could have dropped significantly without proper leadership and someone to watch over it.

If you place fewer expectations on others, and more ones on yourself when it comes to estate and succession planning, things will be much easier. Take accountability for all that you are building up and make sure there's a plan in place for your business when you are gone.

Should All the Pieces of the Pie Be the Same Size?

When you're reviewing your assets and determining how you would like your estate divided, think carefully about how you allocate things. For some people, the answer is simple: Well, we have three kids so we'll just divide everything into three and everyone should be happy. But, what if one of your kids has invested significantly more time and effort in supporting you through your senior years? Should they get more? How will they feel if they know they gave of their time and skills and emotions, and put off things they wanted to do in order to be there for you, only to learn that you do not recognize or appreciate those sacrifices? Or, what if you have a more complicated family situation, such as multiple children from different relationships, or stepchildren? I realize it's not all about money, but what I'm getting at, is that *there is a difference between splitting things equally versus splitting your assets in a fair way.*

Also, like Leona Helmsley whom I mentioned previously, you may want to leave instructions and something in particular for your beloved pets. After all, they are part of your family as well. Or, maybe you want to leave a portion of your estate to a charitable organization that is meaningful to you. You can't assume that just because people love and care for you, they will know exactly what you want. The point is: not only do you need to determine how you want your assets or businesses divided or passed on, you must also communicate your wishes effectively.

In the Bank of Montreal report referenced earlier, 60% of those surveyed felt assets should be divided equally between children, or that children should receive an equal value from the estate. But when The Bank of Montreal asked individuals whose parents had already passed if they felt their parents distributed their estates in a fair way, the results came out as follows:

Yes. Everyone received an equal share.	31%
Yes. Not equal, but this was justified.	11%
No. Items of value given specifically.	7%
No. Taxes led to unequal distribution.	10%
No. But it was my parents' choice and I accept it.	18%
No. It was my parents' choice and I disapprove.	4%
None of the above.	31%

In our family business, my husband and I have actively worked in it and contributed for over 25 years. My brother, on the other hand, is not actively involved in the family business. He has his own graphic design and animation company. Currently, our family business and investments are held within a holding company. My brother and I each own 50 percent of the common shares. Does this sound like a fair arrangement? For some it may seem so, but to be honest, I don't think so. Equal yes, but fair?

I think our shares should be contingent upon how much we are contributing. So, I've had to talk to my parents and my brother about how I feel. It's a bit awkward, and the last thing I want is for them to think I'm selfish. But what is more important to me is that if I am working hard to support the business and making sacrifices in my own life, I feel I deserve to have a greater piece of the pie. In addition, I think my husband's contribution should also be recognized, which is why we are now talking about perhaps making some structural changes to the ownership of the business. Keep in mind also that it's not just about money and ownership; it's also about *leadership* in the business. For example, if a 50 percent partner is not active in the business but has equal decision-making ability, this could lead to stalemates and also to circumstances where someone who doesn't understand the business could make misinformed choices.

I've had many talks with my brother, and the good thing is that he is not the type of person who is interested in arguing over control. He acknowledges that he doesn't know much about the family business and that he isn't in a position to offer guidance or input with regards to the direction and strategies we should employ. He is interested in becoming more involved and in understanding the basics of the business just for his own personal knowledge. But we are on the same page in that he would be open to changing the split, due to the fact that our contributions to the business are not even.

At a recent conference I attended—one that was focused on business transitions—I listened to a talk given by the founder of a successful manufacturing business. His father had started the business, and he took over after his father passed away. He stated that he had four children. Three of the children work in the family business, one of which has a spouse who is also in the business, and one child is not involved in the business at all. Over the years, they have made changes to the ownership of the business, allocating larger percentages to those who work in the business, and including the spouse of the one child. The father recognized that not all contributions were equal, so when he divided up his business, he did what made sense for his family.

In other cases, you will find that there is a disparity in wealth when it comes to family members and that wealthier ones may be willing to give up their share of the inheritance, or part of it, to family members who need it more. Again, every family will have a unique situation, so it's a matter of developing an estate and succession plan that you (and other family members) think is fair.

Transition the Wealth, Not Just the Business or Assets

If you leave a business behind for your family and they don't know how to run or manage it, you have left them a huge headache and a burden that they will have to deal with. Often when we think about creating a legacy, we focus on building and growing. But beyond that, we leave the transition to fate, and in doing so, we risk losing everything we have worked so hard to build.

How can we transition the *wealth* and not just a business or a bunch of assets? We can do this by planning ahead and developing exit strategies that will allow us or our families to capitalize on our years of hard work and to cash out if need be. In this way, it is possible to transition wealth to the next generation by providing them with financial resources to pursue their own interests, to continue to grow the pot, and to pass it on to the next generation.

My son Ethan wants to pursue a career in sports medicine. He hopes to be able to work with athletes and provide guidance and therapy to help them prevent, or recover from, injury. He's only 17, so his plans may change a few times over the years. But at least I know he hopes to pursue a career in a field completely unrelated to our family business. Knowing this allows me to begin having conversations with him about what he can expect if anything were to happen to Ron and/or me.

We have shared with him the basics regarding the real estate investments that we hold, and we have let him know that they will be passed on to him. We've told him that we are working to structure our real estate investment company so it will be in a position to be sold if the time ever came when he would not be interested in overseeing it. The choice is his. We are simply ensuring that he has options available that will tie into his own future plans.

In addition, we talk to him about our family holding company and what will pass on to him. We also outline the responsibilities and options that he would have so that he is clear on things at an early stage and is aware that he will need to communicate openly with other family members, given that this family holding company is owned jointly. We want him to understand, and be prepared to handle, the legacy and inheritance that will be his.

We don't just want to leave behind "stuff." We want to leave behind the value of all that we have worked to create and do it in such a way that he can take it and grow it to the next level using his own unique skills and talents.

A Tale of Things Done Right

There is a way to do things right, and it's as simple as getting it done early and keeping it updated. *Fast and Furious* actor Paul Walker set a good example of doing things right. He died at the early age of 40 in a car accident. Many people at that point in their lives haven't done any estate planning because they don't think it's a priority, but Walker got his affairs in order at the age of 28. He had left very simple instructions in his will, leaving his fortune to his daughter through a trust of which her mother would be the guardian. By doing so, his estate was settled fairly quickly and this allowed his family peace, rather than legal paperwork and arguments during their time of grieving. (Source: everplans.com article – "7 Crucial Estate Planning Lessons from Famous People.")

Communicating your wishes is an integral part of estate planning and it's the key that ensures the legacy you leave behind is exactly what you wanted. In this chapter we took a look at the impact of not communicating clearly. As we move on to the next chapter, we will continue to talk about communication but will shift the focus to the nuances of intergenerational communication.

≡CHAPTER≡

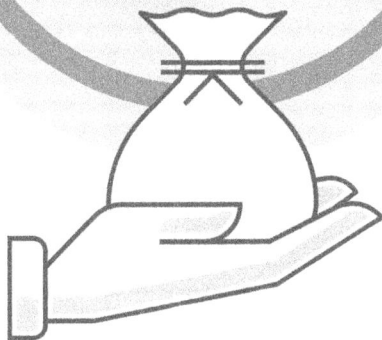

CHAPTER

7

Communicate Openly – Love, Obligation, & Guilt – Generational Differences

Several years ago, my son was working on a project for school and he asked me what year I was born. When I told him, his eyes opened wide in disbelief as he said, "OMG, Mom, that's the olden days. Did you even have cars back then?" As I went on to explain how things were when I was growing up, he pondered how we could have survived "back then" without technology. I chuckled as he took it all in, but I also noted how different our outlooks on life were.

Every generation has a different outlook on life. You can see it in their actions, how they talk, even in their nonverbal cues. Then, throw in a family business each generation values differently, and the process of intergenerational estate and succession planning can be tricky, so it's important to take the time to understand everyone's point of view.

Love, obligation, and guilt is a recurring theme throughout this book because it is *emotion* that hits us hardest as humans. The actual process and steps involved in estate and succession planning can be straightforward and rather boring. But the *impact* on us, and on our family members, is often profound.

We often make choices and do things because of how they make us *feel*. Much can be learned by simply listening and trying to understand where someone is coming from, and what they might be feeling, rather that interrupting and trying to force your viewpoint on them.

Conflict sometimes arises because we do things for different emotional reasons. When a child is young, a parent might coddle the child and be overprotective because they love them and want them to be safe. But that same action at a later date, though still done out of love, may cause a child to feel angry and resentful because it makes them feel restricted. So, it's the same action but the emotional response is different.

This doesn't change much when we deal with our family as we age. Keep this in mind when working through the emotional minefield you may have to cross when dealing with estate and succession planning.

Family – The Tie that Binds

My dad grew up in the Philippines in a small provincial village. His family didn't have much but he lived life to the fullest every day. Always intrigued by the natural world around him, he was a talented student, and I think much of this had to do with his never-ending curiosity. He's still like that today. He often tells me about one of his favorite uncles who inspired and encouraged him to reach for the stars.

Opportunity knocked when my dad was 18. He had the chance to enlist with the US Navy and he eagerly did so. He quickly learned a lot during that phase of his life. Discipline, teamwork, perseverance, and many other qualities were reinforced during his time in the military. He often attributes his success as an entrepreneur to the skills he picked up in the Navy.

After serving in the Navy for several years, my dad ended up in the United States and he applied for a student visa to get his undergraduate degree. My mom at the time was working as a nurse in Minneapolis. My dad was accepted by many schools, but in the end, he accepted the invitation to attend the University of Toronto. My parents settled there and they got married. Dad finished his bachelor's degree in engineering and graduated with honors. Then he was accepted at McMaster University where he completed his Ph.D. in Nuclear Physics.

After graduating, my dad was fortunate to get a job with Ontario Hydro. He worked there for over 30 years and eventually retired in the early nineties. Upon retiring, he, along with some of his peers, decided to start a business in the flow measurement industry. It took many years to get the business up and running profitably, and over the years the partners started dropping out one by one until it was only my dad left.

Seeking My Parents' Approval

Today, we celebrate having been in business for over 25 years. Over the years, my dad always encouraged me to be an active part of the business. And wanting to be a good daughter, I was often swayed to do the things I thought would make my parents proud and happy. I was a true people pleaser to the point where sometimes I wasn't sure what I really wanted myself. Whereas my brother never really got the same push to join the family business nor did he express interest in participating in it. Some days when I talk to my dad about the future of the business, he says we should start grooming my son, Ethan, to take over. But Ethan has no interest in such a role, and I would never force it on him or guilt him into taking it on. Think about the *love, obligation, and guilt* in this paragraph alone.

A Business Built with Love

My dad built this business up from scratch and put his whole heart and soul into it. His is a story of hard work, perseverance, beating the odds, and dedication. He created a business that provides cash flow and financial freedom to our family, but it has taken a lot of joint effort, sacrifice, and work to keep it going. The stress and hard work involved with running a business can be overwhelming, and I've seen many families fall apart under the weight of a business.

My dad built his company in order to provide for us. He invested his time and effort to make it great because he loves us. He sees this business as a gem that belongs to our family, and I know that deep inside he has always hoped that it was something that could be passed along from generation to generation. He loves this company because it's his passion and because of what it has done for our family. But other family members may have their own ideas. And this is where there can be complications if the issue is not properly handled.

The Pull of Obligation and Guilt

Although I have other interests and aspirations, I find myself constantly coming back to AMAG. At times I find myself angry, frustrated, and resentful. Sometimes, I feel I've been living my dad's dream and that I've been building up and sustaining what he has created by setting aside some of my *personal* goals and dreams. And oddly, at other times I feel my heart filled with love and gratitude for what the business has provided for us. Not only has it been financially rewarding, it has also given me a strong foundation that has allowed me to become a strong, successful, and inspirational leader. I wouldn't be where I am today without those experiences, contacts, and resources. A dichotomy of emotion. Strange how that works, isn't it?

The challenge with an intergenerational family business is learning how to deal with different perspectives and how to manage the flurries of random emotions that come along with it. Having multiple options for discussion is important in respecting and honoring all parties involved.

This is why communication and planning are so important. We covered those topics in the previous chapter, and I can't emphasize enough that if you love your family, you will invest the time and effort in ensuring that you create an estate and succession plan that takes into account their interests, goals, and passions. When planning and communicating, take the time to shift your focus and try to understand their points of view.

That complicated mixture of love, obligation, and guilt will always be around, but if you learn how to manage it well and move forward even if you have conflicting feelings, you (and your family) will be much farther ahead. There is no "solution" to the pull of obligation and guilt. All you can do is be aware that you have these feelings, remember that there is also love, and know that you can manage the mixture. It may take some difficult conversations but remind yourself that love is always part of the mix.

What Role Do You Play?

Estate and succession planning often spans across multiple generations and it's critical that these generations work together. Each family is different, but there are common roles that need to be filled and somehow people seem to naturally take on the roles that highlight their strengths. Understanding the role you play within your family and how to best interact with the other family members becomes easier when you take the time to learn what motivates each of them.

When we are young, our parents take on the responsibility of caring for us and putting things in place to ensure that if anything happens to them, we will be cared for. As we grow older and become independent, things start to shift and we begin doing this type of planning for our own families. A little further down the road, as parents begin to age, many of us find ourselves spending time helping and supporting them at the same time as we are raising our own families.

Being able to remain fluid and to grow with each other is essential to smooth transitions. I learned early on that being rigid and inflexible doesn't lead to positive results. Instead, take the time to listen and understand what is important to those around you.

In every family, you will see a number of different roles emerge. From my own observations, I see a few key roles that are consistent:

The Alpha – Leader of the pack – Usually takes the initiative when it comes to important discussions or decisions. Often this is the primary breadwinner and the person who oversees the family's financial activities.

Leader in Training – A family member who is similar to the leader of the pack in that they display similar leadership capabilities and appear to be the natural successor.

Support Member – A family member (or members) who primarily play a support role. Support members often require some guidance from the leader when it comes to family affairs. A support member often oversees day-to-day household, emotional, and family-related tasks.

The Rebel – A family member who actively chooses to be different, to rebel, and sometimes to cause conflict just for the sake of doing so.

Dependents – Those family members (usually children, the elderly, or anyone who is ill) who are dependent and not fully able to contribute.

In the early years, my dad was the leader of the pack. When it came to *his* parents (my grandparents), he helped provide important input and financial resources to ensure they were well cared for as they aged. Within our own family, my dad was the head honcho leading us and building up our family nest egg by accumulating wealth, investing wisely, and striving to grow his business. He put structures and mechanisms in place to protect what he was building and he began the initial planning of how things would be passed along.

My mom, also a strong and influential individual, took on the role of the primary support person. She often did what was necessary to ensure that my dad could stay focused. First, she worked full time supporting him while he was in the university so that he could finish his Ph.D. and get a great job, and then she worked part time while raising us children to ensure that my dad could build his career. And lastly, she was there to support my dad as he built the family business. Today, my mom plays an integral role in keeping everyone in order and maintaining peace in the family. She ensures our emotional needs are met and she forces us to take time to step away sometimes so we can rest, relax, and rejuvenate. She is also the one who has been the primary instigator of getting all our estate and succession planning in order.

Growing up, I played the role of the leader in training. For much of my childhood, my education and experience were geared toward grooming me to follow in my parents' footsteps and achieve success. I was encouraged to develop skills that would help with growing and supporting our family business. Now, as my parents age, I find myself moving into the role of the leader of the pack and taking charge when it comes to ensuring our family legacy carries on.

Similar to my mom, my brother plays a supporting role. He is not active in our family business and instead has a business of his own. When it comes to family affairs, he typically doesn't take the initiative to tackle what needs to be done, but he always steps up in a supporting role to help out when needed.

Both my brother and I have children, and over time their roles will become defined. They each have different natural talents and abilities, and as they use and further develop their strengths, they will fall into the roles that best suit them. If all goes as planned, and our family legacy continues, my son and his cousins will work together to snowball what we have created and develop a path to continue to transition this wealth to future generations.

My own life over the last three to five years has been a bit of a whirlwind. As my parents age and my own child grows up, I find myself in this weird space where I'm shifting what I do to accommodate the needs of our family. I have stepped away from the day-to-day operations of AMAG and my husband has stepped up to take on the role of President.

Meeting regularly with my family and working through the things we need to sort out over the next few years has been very beneficial for me. I know that all the time we spend doing this will pay off in the long run. I am excited to work together to ensure that the legacy we are creating will be sustainable for generations to come.

I also hope that we will leave behind valuable lessons and inspiration regarding entrepreneurship, leadership, personal growth, finances, accounting, and personal finance. It is this wisdom, knowledge, and planning that will ensure a successful and lasting legacy, one that will make a difference for many years to come.

Intergenerational Communication

Find a Common Language

When it comes to communicating across different generations, it's important to realize that sometimes we're on different pages when it comes to understanding technology and new trends and so we need to find a common language that everyone is comfortable with.

For instance, when working with my parents to help them organize their net worth statement and related backup material, I created a simple spreadsheet that can be updated very easily. I always print out hard copies for them because they don't always trust technology. And so, for their comfort and peace of mind, having a tangible piece of paper they can feel, touch, and see makes them happy.

I also make sure that when we have to share information, we do it in many different formats. Email is probably the easiest and fastest way to communicate a lot of information to my whole family at one time. However, I often follow up with a phone call or text to make sure that my parents received it and that they understand what is going on. People have different preferences on how they like to be communicated with so being mindful of this allows for our messages to be better received by others.

I have also learned that patience is a hugely important trait. Sometimes, with complex concepts and situations, I have to repeat things multiple times in different ways. Even though I may fully understand what I'm talking about, I have to make sure that I am clearly communicating it with the rest of my family. Sometimes, this can be frustrating but taking a deep breath and remaining calm helps me to get the message across more effectively than if I might sound irritated or impatient.

My communication style varies depending on who I'm talking to. For instance, I use a different approach when talking to my parents, husband, or brother versus when I'm communicating with my son and nephews, which requires a different approach. For the younger generation, concepts need to be simplified and presented at a level they will understand. Also, they are so well versed in technology that using YouTube videos is often the best way to help them learn the concepts more readily. Sometimes, coming up with analogies that will resonate with my son can be tricky because the things I refer to may be so far back in history that they don't make sense to him. So, I try to find stories or analogies using topics that he will understand, such as sports, music, or current affairs. As Ron and I age, it will be important to keep the lines of communication open and be clear about the path we are agreeing to as a family.

Things like documenting what you talk about, getting people to sign off on important decisions, and getting outside advice when you aren't sure about the technicalities of something can be important.

Find a Guide

Would you try to trek through the Amazon jungle on your own? Of course not. You would likely hire a guide who knows the way, understands the inherent dangers, has survival skills, and may even know some handy shortcuts. A guide will help you safely make your way to your destination.

Estate and succession planning can be a complex journey and sometimes it helps to have an objective guide present to help guide your family conversations.

My family has found it useful to retain the services of a coach or mediator. We have regular meetings with our coach, Grace. She guides us through the process of whatever it is we are trying to accomplish. Having an intermediary is a great way to minimize conflict and keep everyone focused on the task at hand. A good coach or intermediary will keep you on track and hold you accountable to the things you agree to complete.

Understanding and Respecting Each Other's Point of View

I've learned that you can't *change* people or their point of view, all you can do is to try to *influence* them. Then *they* will decide if they want to change anything. I think you get the most out of a situation if you take the time to stop and really, really listen to what they are saying. And then after you listen, take even more time to try to understand where they are coming from and perhaps why.

When it comes to estate and succession planning, it's important to understand that your family members have their own reasons and motivations for doing things a certain way. Perhaps, your parents want to structure their affairs in a way that doesn't make sense to you. It is their life, their plan, and at the end of the day, their choice.

I have had conversations with a number of my peers and it isn't unusual to hear people complaining about what their parents have done, or how they don't think things are fair, or how there is an ongoing battle amongst family members because of very different belief systems.

I've even listened to a friend complain about their parents spending and enjoying their money because they feel that this will reduce the amount of their inheritance. Seriously, true story.

One of my mentors shared a story with me about her own family situation. Her father passed away unexpectedly and now she is working through some estate and succession planning to get her own affairs in order, as well as helping her mother to also do some planning. In a survey I sent out, I asked what issues and challenges people face while going through the estate and succession planning process, and she highlighted several issues:

1. When family members have a different relationship with money and this creates conflict. For instance, short-term vs. long-term view, spender vs. saver, entitlement vs. responsibility.

2. Difficulty knowing the wishes of the deceased person because their will is vague or unclear.

3. Assigning key responsibilities as trustee and executor when the chosen person does not have the skills to carry out those duties.

These three challenges are just a few examples where taking the time to understand differing points of view may be helpful in working through issues. You many never come to total *agreement*, but if you can learn to accept that and work together to come to an acceptable *compromise*, this may be a satisfactory result. Simply arguing about these points will lead nowhere, so it is better to acknowledge that you may never agree and then move forward.

In my own family, we've had some pretty deep conversations about the future of AMAG. I know this business means a lot to my dad. I sense that he had hoped this was a business that could be passed down from generation to generation and continue to be owned and operated by our family. His perspective comes from the fact that he was the founder, has an emotional attachment to the business, and created it out of a desire to support and take care of our family. In his mind, it's a gift created out of love and I absolutely respect that. He often says he's open to other options, although I always sense a bit of resistance if we discuss exit strategies. I may not have the same feeling about the company but I have come to understand and respect my dad's point of view.

I, on the other hand, am open to exit strategies for the business. Perhaps because I'm not the founder and it's not something that I created myself, I am a little more detached. Growing up in an entrepreneurial family, I have developed a love for business, but I also see it as being transactional in nature. I look at AMAG, see the potential to maximize its value, and believe that it would be beneficial to do so in order to make it attractive to potential buyers. Doing this wouldn't make the success of the business dependent on family members to carry it forward, especially if they may not have the desire or skill to do so. It doesn't mean that I want to sell the business today but rather that I want to ensure it's sellable and attractive to potential buyers if we choose to go that route.

When it comes to the real estate investment company Ron and I own, I feel the same way. I thought as a founder I would have a strong attachment to keeping it in the family. But just like AMAG, I enjoy the opportunity to grow it, maximize its value, and put structures in place so it can be easily sold down the road should my son not be interested in overseeing it. I would be thrilled for him to continue to grow it but only if that's what he wants. If his preference is to pursue other opportunities in life, then I would be happy to work with him to sell the business and allow him to benefit from the wealth that comes out of it.

I have talked to many fellow business owners who have spent years building up successful businesses. When I ask what their plans are when they retire, many say that they will just close up shop. Just like that—shut the doors and walk away. But what about all the value that has been built up over the years? Many of them don't realize that with some planning and restructuring, they could exit their business by selling it, and then use those funds to retire or to invest the funds in whatever they see next in their life.

I sometimes do brief sessions with fellow business owners to help them hash out a plan regarding what steps they might need to take in order to make their businesses attractive to potential buyers. Sometimes they don't realize the value they have built up nor do they think anyone would be willing to pay for it. Others think that it's far too much work to sell a business. But once we break it all down, they realize that the time and effort put into maximizing their business and preparing it for an eventual sale is minimal compared to the benefits that will result for them and their families.

Take some time to think about what small changes you could make in your business today that would help make it sellable down the road. Books, such as *Built to Sell* by John Warrillow, are great guides for doing this. They will tell you in detail what buyers look for when buying a business. Understanding the perspective of a buyer will give you helpful clues regarding what it would take to make your business attractive to them.

It's Okay to Be Emotional (and/or uncomfortable)

Estate and succession planning is an emotional process. Thinking about your loved ones passing away or getting ill is not a pleasant topic. And expressing how you feel about estate and succession planning can be stressful if you and your family members are not all on the same page. Just know that it's absolutely okay to have different opinions or to be emotional as you go through the process. You don't have to hide your emotions or hold them in. In fact, discussing your emotions is healthy, and by showing how you truly feel, it may be easier to create understanding and compassion with one another.

It has been heartbreaking to see things change for my parents as they age, and sad to think about the day that they will no longer be here. But as much as it's a topic we'd rather avoid, we do discuss it so we can help them leave behind a legacy that they are proud of.

Conversations about the future of the family business have been emotional and sometimes uncomfortable, but the end result of open communication is that we are putting processes and strategies in place that respect my parents' desires and that also respect the fact that my brother, my husband, and I have our own goals, dreams, and passions that we want to pursue.

Many of us struggle with this juggling act as we prepare for the transition of wealth. And many of us are overseeing a family business, helping our parents more frequently as they age, managing our own households, and at the same time trying not to lose sight of our own goals, dreams, and passions. Some days it feels like there isn't much time left to breathe. Not only is it physically tiring, it's also emotionally draining.

Over the past few months, I've shared with my family how I feel about things. There are times when my frustration and emotion flare to the surface, and I used to feel bad about that. Now, I realize that it's necessary to be honest about how I feel and also to communicate my feelings once in awhile.

In the past, I would have held in my feelings. I probably wouldn't have said anything and I would have just carried on, even if I was frustrated and upset about things. But, living like that was causing me to feel depressed and to experience some horrible bouts of anxiety. People saw me as the strong one who took care of things, but inside I was beginning to crack.

The biggest lesson I learned from that period was that communication is key for *everyone's* health and well-being. In addition, communicating in a way that can be heard and respected is a skill that one needs to develop, especially when dealing with emotional and sensitive topics. It takes practice and it begins with being able to open up and speak your mind while still being respectful of those around you. By opening up and expressing my feelings, I am happy to say that I have been able to get my message across to my family, and we are now working together as a team to make it a win-win for everyone.

Feel the Emotion and Do It Anyway

Many of you may be avoiding estate and succession planning because it is a sensitive and emotional topic.

My advice is: Don't worry about being emotional. Just face your emotions and get busy with putting your affairs in order. There's no sense in trying to sweep this topic under the rug—because one day that rug may get pulled out from under you and you'll end up sitting right on top of the mess you tried to sweep away.

3 Tips for Getting Through an Emotional Conversation

1. Be prepared. Take the time to think about what message you are trying to convey before you have the conversation. When you're clear about what you are communicating, it is easier to stay on track and you are less likely to get caught up in a whirlwind of emotions.

2. Be aware. Understand that you are not the only one with emotions. Take stock of how the others around you are feeling as you move through the conversation and give them space and time to deal with their emotions.

3. Step away if it gets too overwhelming. It's okay to stop and take a break. Sometimes giving everyone a little time to absorb things is helpful. Then set a time to continue the conversation later.

Trust me, trying to go through estate and succession planning as an *afterthought*—when someone has already gotten ill or passed away—can be a nightmare. Grieving takes a toll on you and makes it hard to even think straight, so take action *now* and protect everything you have worked so hard to build up.

≡CHAPTER≡

Yield - Practical Ways to Maximizing Wealth

Have Your Cake and Eat It Too (but don't forget to leave some for your family)

Charlene owns a successful cake-making company called Cake Addicts, which she started with a partner a few years ago. She has a full-time job, but she started this part-time business because she enjoys making cakes. To be honest, I never knew how much work went into making a cake until I listened to her explain the process. Not to mention that there are moments when the whole thing will collapse if you don't handle it properly. No wonder I don't make a cake very often! However, building a business, growing your investments, and living your life so that you can leave a legacy is a lot like making a cake.

Would it make sense to you to carefully plan out the list of required ingredients, go to the store to purchase them, follow a detailed process to mix the batter, bake it, and then spend hours decorating it—only to never take a bite, throw it in the garbage, or let it sit and go bad? Of course not! Naturally, the next step after creating a beautiful cake would be to enjoy it with family and friends. Or in Charlene's case, deliver it to your customer in order to get paid.

Similarly, in life, you presumably have acquired assets. Maybe you have a nest egg or a business that you have been growing. As with the cake, you need to think about what was the point of creating it.

Exit Options for Your Business

Oddly, when it comes to their business, many people forget about the end game. They work so hard all their lives to "make their cake," but they don't have a plan with regards to what to do with it after it's baked. Some people tell me that they just do what they do because they enjoy it and because it pays their bills, but when they are done, they figure they'll just close up shop. If this is what you really want, I can't say it's wrong. However, wouldn't it be nice to be able to exit your business or investment and benefit from all the hard work you put into growing it?

If you're an entrepreneur and running a successful business, now would be a good time to start planning when it will be time to eat some of your cake and/or share your cake with others. It's called your *exit strategy*.

If you don't know where to begin, here are a few exit options for you to consider:

Liquidate and close your business when you are ready to retire (or if you become ill).

Sell your business.

Merger or acquisition.

Initial public offering.

Maintain ownership but step away from the day-to-day running of the business. Put a strong, trustworthy management team in place to run your business while you maintain ownership and enjoy the cash flow that it generates.

Throw your business away and do nothing. (Not really an option to choose, but quite often this is a consequence of not planning.)

The main point of all this is that regardless of which option you choose, it would be wise to *maximize* the value of your business so you can enjoy the fruits of your labor.

What's my business worth? Who will steal my business if I don't protect it?

When my dad had his heart attack, I realized that if we hadn't been able to continue running the business, we would have had to either close it or sell it. And if we had chosen to sell it, we would have needed a clear understanding of what it was worth. After all, how can you negotiate when you don't have a clue about what a potential buyer would pay for your business? Do you think the prospective buyer will care that you're dealing with grief and therefore make you the best offer? Of course not!

Here's another simple example: A few years ago, we lost a major tenant in an office building that my family owned. This tenant went bankrupt and suddenly 30 percent of our building was empty! The cash flow we had enjoyed dried up quickly, and we worked diligently with our property manager to get the empty space leased out as soon as possible. But with commercial property, it can sometimes take several months to fill vacancies, and without an adequate reserve fund, many property owners struggle or end up having to sell their property. Shortly after we lost our major tenant, we started getting inquiries as to whether we were planning to sell the property. The vultures were circling and hoping to make the most of our difficult situation.

Thankfully, we had an adequate reserve fund, and with our amazing property managers we were able to turn things around and get this property performing again. We had financial resources, strong management, and the benefit of having run through scenarios such as this before even buying the property. All these things allowed us to protect what we had and send the vultures away.

Over the years that I have worked within our family business, I have found that our focus has always been on the day-to-day operations. It wasn't until we began more actively working on succession planning that we began to focus on *what our business was worth*. According to the *Harvard Business Review*, most entrepreneurs and business owners have an inflated perception of what their business is worth. This is because people tend to place a higher value on things they own versus things that aren't theirs. But forget about what *you* think it's worth; its real value is based on what the market will be willing to pay for it.

Understanding Business Valuation

To start, ask your accountant to go over the concept of business valuation and how it works. Even a simple understanding will allow you to look at your business from a different perspective. In addition to being useful for estate and succession planning purposes, having an updated valuation of your business may be helpful for other reasons. You may need to get some financing for expansion or to cover cash flow issues. Or perhaps you are planning to add shareholders or buy out existing shareholders. In any case, the point is that knowledge is power. By understanding what your business is worth, you will be in a better position to increase its value or to negotiate more effectively with a potential buyer, investor, or shareholder.

Future Earning Power - EBITDA Valuation Multiple

You may have heard the funny word "EBITDA" thrown around, most likely by your accountant. EBITDA is actually an acronym that stands for Earnings Before Interest, Taxes, Depreciation, and Amortization. EBITDA is something you can calculate by pulling items from an income statement; and if you aren't familiar with it, you can ask your accountant to explain it to you.

There are several ways to value a business. Potential buyers, investors, or shareholders will likely look at more than one of these ways when trying to establish the value of your business. I'm not an accountant or business valuation specialist, so I will leave the nitty gritty of how those methods work to your accounting professional. But to help you figure out a ballpark value for your business, I will share some information on the most common method for valuing a business.

Just like any other investment, the value of your business stems largely from its ability to generate a return. In this case, it's all about *earnings*. To figure out the value of your business using this method, you calculate a multiple of EBITDA (earnings before interest, taxes, depreciation, and amortization). The multiplier used for small- to medium-sized businesses is usually in the range of three to six times EBIDTA. This multiplier is a statistically derived ratio based on comparable sales of businesses in the same industry. In addition, the multiple used may be influenced by the size of the business, the management team, goodwill, intellectual property, and any other relevant factors.

Here's a very simplified example to show you how it works:

Andrea runs a small manufacturing company that makes widgets. She has a good client base, and many are repeat customers. She has a staff of 15 people, she recently hired a Chief Operating Officer to manage the day-to-day operations of the business, and she herself spends most of her time focusing on strategy. Over the years, she has put a solid quality assurance program in place, and she has systematized most of the business to ensure things run smoothly. Over the last few years, her EBITDA has fluctuated at around $350,000. After consulting with her accountants, she understands that the multiple to use would range between 4.5 and 5. With this knowledge, she can do a quick ballpark calculation to see what her business is worth.

EBITDA: $350,000

Multiplier (specific to small businesses in the widget industry): 4.5

ESTIMATED VALUE OF ANDREA's BUSINESS: $350,000 x 4.5 = $1,575,000

Adjustments to the Calculation

Your EBITDA helps you to get started on the right track to understanding what your business may be worth to a potential buyer. But it's important to note that you may need to make adjustments to your EBITDA calculation in order to take into account the nuances of how you run your business, any debt against the business, and other such factors.

As an example, some business owners don't pay themselves a salary. But if they were to sell the business, the new owners would most likely need to pay someone to run it or they might want a salary themselves. In this instance, a potential buyer would reduce your EBITDA by the salary they would be paying after taking over the business because this would be a more realistic picture of what it is worth. There may be other instances where specific adjustments need to be made, but as I mentioned earlier, these are things best discussed with your accountant.

ACTION: Do you know what your EBITDA is? If not, this would be a great time to stop and take a look at your financial statements. This would also be a good time to touch base with your accountant and at least set up a phone call or meeting to get a feel for what multiplier to use.

Other Factors to Consider

There are obviously many other factors that may make your business more attractive to a potential buyer. Understanding what these factors are and implementing changes today may be very helpful in maximizing the value of your business, so when it comes time to sell, you will be in a stronger position. As you read through these factors, take some time to think about your business and whether you need to make changes or improvements in any of these areas.

Management team – Potential buyers often seek out businesses with a management team in place. It's also helpful if there is a long-term incentive plan in place for the management team to increase the likelihood they will stay on after the business is acquired.

In many small businesses, the owner takes on the role of "management" all on their own. As a business owner, keep in mind that potential buyers will want a smooth transition and may ask you to stay on for a length of time as part of the deal. So, if you plan to fully exit your business in the next few years, you may want to get started on preparing it for sale today. Also, if anything happens to you, and your family is left to sell your business, would it still be valuable to a buyer if you are no longer at the helm? This is why it's important to have others in place so the operation of your business is not fully dependent on *you* being there.

Systems – Having well documented processes and procedures is essential for the successful continuity of your business. Even though things may seem like second nature to you, a new owner will need as much guidance as possible to ensure a successful takeover. Developing procedures and processes for every area of your business is something you should be doing in any case, but if you aren't, I suggest you start today.

Having strong systems in place ensures that even if you become incapacitated or pass away, someone else can take over with minimal disruption to the day-to-day operations of the business.

Think of this as creating a "user's manual" for your business.

Relationships – Much of the value of your business comes from the relationships you have built up with your clients, suppliers, employees, alliance partners, and anyone else you work with. Who owns or manages the relationships within your business? Are you the key to all of these relationships? If so, a potential buyer would likely want you (or whoever holds the key to these relationships) to stay on long enough to help transition these relationships to the individuals who will eventually take over.

Culture – What does your corporate culture look like or feel like? When someone walks into your business, how do you think they will perceive the informal (person-to-person) culture? Does it feel stuffy and closed off? Is it lively and positive? Does it seem like an environment where teamwork is encouraged, or are the staff all isolated behind their desks? Some acquirers may look for companies that share a common culture with their own. Think about it from the buyer's point of view and build up an open, positive, and flexible environment.

Goodwill – Goodwill is an intangible (but important) asset that reflects the value of a company's brand, relationships, customer base, and any patents or proprietary technology. If a potential buyer sees that a company has strong goodwill, they will often be willing to pay a premium for this quality.

When Should You Get Started?

The *best* answer is that you should start working on this when you start your business. But the next best answer is to start thinking about changes and implementing them *today* or as soon as possible. Realistically, the first few years of running a business are usually tough enough. But as years pass and you get closer to wanting to retire or step away, it becomes very important to figure out what you plan to do with your business. As I have already stated, regardless of which option you choose, maximizing the value of your business is a smart strategic move that allows you to reap the rewards of what you've sown.

Maximizing the value of a business is not something you can do overnight. Structuring your business so it is desirable and sellable takes strategic planning, focus, dedication, and a team of professionals to guide you along the way. There are many resources out there that can help you understand some of the steps you should go through when positioning your business for sale. One of the best is *Built To Sell – Creating a Business that Can Thrive Without You*, by John Warrillow. In the book, Mr. Warrillow shares 17 tips to maximize the value of your business. He also includes an implementation guide with eight steps that walk you through the process of selling your business.

Put Yourself in a Buyer's Shoes

When it comes to maximizing the value of your assets or your business, you need to put yourself in the shoes of a prospective buyer. By understanding how they think, what they will be looking for, and what they value most, you will be in a better position to negotiate with them.

Taking the time to understand how an outsider would view your business helps give you a better understanding of what you need to do to make it more attractive and get a fair price.

Do some research as if you were looking to buy a company. If you google "what to look for when buying a business," you will come across many articles and worksheets that will help you understand how a buyer thinks. You can then take this information and use it to review your assets or business and see what work can be done to improve the value of what you have today.

This was one of the most useful things my family did when we were learning about business valuations. We went through articles and websites that shared information on important things to look for when buying a business. Yes, that's right; I spent a lot of time researching as if I was a buyer and not a seller. Looking at things from that point of view opened my mind to how others would perceive our business. Also, with help from our accountants, we had the opportunity to meet with a small company that specializes in buying companies such as ours. It was a friendly conversation aimed at allowing us to learn about the key things a buyer would want to see. If you ever get the opportunity to do this, I would highly recommend it. It will give you a lot of insight into changes or new processes that you may want to implement in your business to make it more valuable.

ACTION: Even if you don't plan to retire or to sell your business anytime soon, take an hour or two to search for information on what buyers look for when buying a business. And if you are serious about making some lasting changes to maximize value, pick up a copy of John Warrillow's book, *Built to Sell*, as mentioned earlier.

Maximizing the Value of Your Investments

Real Estate – The Devil Is in the Details

As a real estate investor, I have often seen situations where a big life event occurs (divorce, sudden illness, death, inheritance) and owners sell a property for much less than market value. This is partly due to a sense of urgency and haste. I mentioned the vultures circling my property earlier when we were going through a tough time.

In North America, the rate of home ownership has varied over the years but has typically stayed within the range of 63.9 percent to 69.2 percent, as found in tables provided by the website, www.tradingeconomics.com. For many individuals, their home is their most valuable asset. Over the years, as the mortgage is paid down and the property value appreciates, homeowners are able to enjoy watching the equity in their property grow. Often, properties pass from one spouse or partner to another in the event of a death. In other cases, parents leave their home to their children, and it's up to the children to either sell the property, rent it out, or move into it.

Property values are usually driven by comparable sales. This is the average sell price of the properties that have sold in the same area within the last few months. Although it may seem that maximizing the value of your home is up to the market and out of your hands, there are some very basic things you can do to help boost the desirability of your home and make it more appealing to buyers (should you decide to sell at some point.) These include:

Good recordkeeping and documentation.

Proper maintenance and upkeep of all equipment, electrical, plumbing, etc.

Upgrade/update as required to keep it in good condition.

Go green.

Keep it clean.

It sounds simple, but sadly, homes are sometimes not well maintained, and when they are passed on or have to be sold, a lot of value can be lost.

Sometimes the property just hasn't been well maintained, and with the stress of the situation the individuals tasked with selling the home don't want to, or are unable to, spend a bit of time and money updating and fixing the property to maximize its value. If you simply maintain, update, and keep things in good order, you can feel more confident that the value you are building up will be retained and passed on when the time comes.

Additional Investment Properties

If you also own investment properties, there are steps you can take to maximize the value of your portfolio. The value of your real estate investment portfolio is influenced largely by how much income it produces. So, in addition to the suggestions for maintaining your personal home, I would suggest taking the following steps with your investment portfolio:

1. Implement rent increases when you can.
2. Be a hawk and manage your expenses wisely.
3. Work with experienced and reputable property managers to oversee your portfolio.
4. Meet with your managers on a regular basis to get updates and check on how things are going.
5. Keep your properties well maintained and upgraded to attract and retain good tenants.
6. Work with a good accountant to make sure the financials and tax returns for your properties are done correctly.
7. Highest and best use—can your property be modified, converted, or changed in order to maximize its potential?
8. Prune your portfolio as required. In other words, get rid of under-performing properties when necessary and replace them with profitable ones.

As your portfolio grows over time, make sure to have regular conversations with your lawyer, accountant, and estate planning professional re-garding the best way to hold your properties from a liability, tax, and estate and succession planning standpoint. Putting in place the best structures to hold your portfolio will be beneficial in the long run and will allow for a smoother transition and hopefully a successful and profitable sale down the road.

Other Assets

You probably also have some of your wealth invested in mutual funds, stocks, bonds, options, GICs or other such financial investment vehicles. Often people hold these types of investments inside their registered retire-ment accounts.

I know a handful of people who are very active in overseeing these types of financial investments. They understand the nuances of the vehicles they are invested in and work closely with their financial advisors to ensure their portfolios are performing to their satisfaction.

But, the majority of people I've spoken with seem to leave the manage-ment of these assets up to their financial planner and just hope for the best. They take a passive role. Many don't have the knowledge or desire to want to actively oversee these investments, so they rely on a third party and hope that their funds are being well managed. Obviously, this isn't the greatest strategy for maximizing your wealth and ensuring your hard-earned funds are working for you.

I've been very guilty of this myself. Although my investment portfolio is largely made up of real estate related investments, I do have registered retirement funds invested in mutual funds, and to be honest I rarely even look at the statements. If anything, I meet with my banker once a year, review my investment profile, listen to his suggestions, and then make changes if they seem necessary. More recently, aside from the registered funds that I contribute to regularly (to be able to take advantage of our company matching policy), I have made the decision to keep most of my funds invested in things that I am familiar with and that I understand.

I have a few basic tips that may help to ensure that you are getting the best bang for your buck when it comes to your financial investments.

Review regularly: meet with your financial advisor/planner, and come prepared with questions so you can become more familiar with what you are invested in.

Ask questions: if you aren't satisfied with the returns you are getting, speak up and ask about alternatives that may better suit your objectives.

Understand the costs related to your investments: take some time to learn about the expenses related to the management of your portfolio (management fees, etc.), and if you find the fees too high, consider shopping around.

Knowledge is power: take time to learn about investing in general; there are many good books and resources available.

Keep your funds invested in things that you understand.

Do what works best for you: don't just jump into something because everyone else is doing it; stop and think about whether a specific investment meets your needs.

One thing I learned from my parents a long time ago is that it's one thing to know how to *make* money but it's a whole other world to know how to hang on to it and get it working for you. Don't take the risk of letting someone else dissipate your hard-earned fortune. Or in other words, check in on your cake while it's baking.

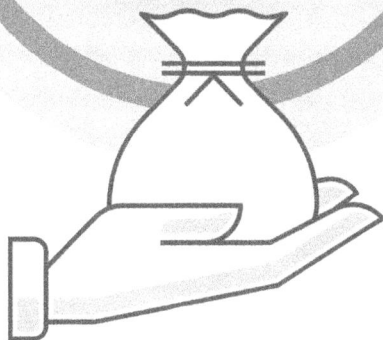

≡CHAPTER≡

9

Passing the Baton to Win a Medal

Imagine training your whole life to get to the Olympics to participate in the 4x100 meter relay. You've invested substantial time, effort, and money on coaches and training to become an elite athlete who can run like the wind. But even though you knew you were participating in a sport where at some point you would have to pass the baton on to another runner, you didn't spend much time practicing with another athlete, or working on your timing, or how you would hand over the baton.

Then, as you embark on the path to your moment of glory, you arrive at your event in front of a world stage, run the best leg you've ever run, but then clumsily drop the baton before it is securely in the hands of the next runner. That small hiccup results in you having to watch all of the other runners pass you by as you realize that everything you trained so hard for is now ending in failure. How upsetting would it be to realize that all you had to do was spend a bit of time practicing with your teammate and you would have had a gold medal.

Actions Speak Louder than Words

Thinking and talking about your situation is one thing but you'll only see results once you take concrete action. Many of the people I've interviewed tell me they've thought about or talked about estate and succession planning but they haven't taken any action or put anything in place. In the survey I once sent out to a group of my peers, asking why people hadn't done any planning, one of the common answers was, "It just hasn't been enough of a priority yet." Sometimes it's worded in different ways, but for the most part it appears that many individuals feel that estate and succession planning is a task that is something to be done *at a later time*.

That scares me.

Because when it does become a priority, it's going to be because something bad has happened. You've dropped the baton, which means it's too late to work on it.

Tips for a Smooth Transition

1. Review any existing wills or other estate planning documentation already in place. Determine if they need to be updated (especially if you've had any major life changes such as marriage, children, divorce, etc.).

2. Review the beneficiaries on your investment accounts or insurance policies to make sure those beneficiaries are still the ones you want in place.

3. Have your finances and related paperwork organized and up to date. As discussed earlier, update your net worth statement, and document what you have, where it's held, and who has access to it.

4. Determine how you want your estate to be distributed. If you have a more complex family situation, will you be including exes or previous family members? Other things to think about are family heirlooms and other valuables with sentimental value. Who will they go to?

5. Will you be leaving some of your estate to a charitable or other organization?

6. If you have a business, who will take over your ownership position or look after other related details?

7. Simplify. Review what you have in place and clear out any clutter and unnecessary complexities. Close inactive accounts.

8. Be clear on how you want things handled if you become ill or incapacitated, and make sure you have your legal documents in order and have appointed someone to act on your behalf. Talk to your family about the way you want things handled so nothing comes as a shock or surprise to them.

9. Be clear about your wishes for your funeral and service. You may

want to consider visiting a funeral home to ask about preplanning and paying for things in advance so your family doesn't have to be burdened with these tasks while they are grieving.

10. Communicate with your family members *early and often*. I can't emphasize this one enough!

11. Select an executor whom you trust to take care of your wishes as you have specified.

12. If you have younger children, make sure you have already spoken to the person who would be their legal guardian and that you have documented this. Be sure that the legal guardian or guardians you have chosen are willing and capable and ensure that financial resources will be available to them while they are taking care of your children.

13. What about pets? Who will care for your pets in the event of your illness or death? Will you allocate funds for their care?

14. Work with a team to create the legal documents needed to summarize your estate and succession plan.

Go Back to the Beginning with the End in Mind

All the way back in Chapter 5, we talked about beginning with the end in mind. It's useful to refer back to that and think about what things will look like in the ideal future that you have pictured. Then think about the estate and succession planning issues that need to be addressed so your desired scenario will come to pass. Make sure to briefly document your future plans so when you meet with your team of professionals, they can suggest the best way to set things up to accommodate your growth plans.

To put it simply, structure your estate and succession planning to allow for your expected growth.

For Entrepreneurs and Business Owners

As a business owner, it's important to be clear on the exit options you are considering. Assuming you aren't a vampire and won't be able to run your business forever, you need to figure out things such as:

Who will take over ownership of the business?

If you have a partner(s) in the business, what arrangements have you made with them? For instance, if you plan for your shares to go to your spouse or other family member, are your business partners okay with this?

Who will take over leadership of the business? Is this person already working within the organization, or is it someone you will need to bring in and groom for the position? At what point do you think this would need to happen?

Do you plan to sell the business at a certain time and enjoy the fruits of your labor (or pass this wealth on to your family)?

Is the business set up and running in a manner that would be appealing to future buyers? Do you even know who would be on your list of potential buyers?

These are only a few of the questions you need to address when it comes to your business. Maybe you have spent time thinking and talking about them, but as mentioned before, there comes a time when you need to take some concrete action toward putting a succession plan in place.

Who's running the next leg of the race?

One of the main factors to consider is: To whom are you passing the baton? In many cases, people's plans include having everything go to their spouse. Beyond that, they plan for things to transition to their children. How they decide to split things among their children may vary, but for the most part, the bulk of their estate will eventually pass to the next generation. For those who don't have children, many opt to have their assets distributed amongst family members and/or close friends and some include charity organizations.

There are so many different situations, some more complicated that others. For instance, in the case of divorce, remarriage, children from different spouses, estranged children, and other situations, your planning and the communication of your plans can be more complex and perhaps more emotional. Again, this is why it is important to take dedicated time to think things through and communicate with your family members *before* you begin putting together your framework. You end up with a much better plan if you invest a bit of time and effort up front.

For entrepreneurs and business owners, your estate plan should also include a succession plan for your business. Not only do you need to be thinking about who will take over your share of the ownership, if you have been the leader and visionary for the company, you also need to think about who will be next in line to take on this hugely important role.

A Successful Second-Generation Family Business

For family business owners, a common strategy is to have the business pass from one generation to the next. However, according to statistics from the Family Business Institute, only 30 percent of family businesses survive past the second generation, and these failures are often due to in-fighting among family members. If intergenerational ownership and operation of your business is what you want, then as a family you should all be in agreement and support the planned transition. If there is any uncertainty around this, it is best to begin communicating early on.

Here are a few stories, shared with me by some of my peers, that may help get you thinking more about the different scenarios available to you when it comes to passing the baton.

Tales from the Trenches - Real Life Estate and Succession Planning Scenarios

I have a good friend (we'll call him Bill) who owns a successful training company. The company was founded by his father in the 1970s, and Bill has basically worked in the business all his life. Both Bill and his father share a passion for what they do, so it was a win-win situation in that they shared a common desire to carry on this family business together. Bill also has a sister who has helped out in the business as well but not anywhere near the extent that Bill has.

At a certain point, Bill's father made the decision to step away from the day-to-day operations of the business. At this time, Bill stepped up and bought the business from his father. It was a very smooth transition of ownership and leadership. Bill's father still helps out in the business, and he feels comfortable that the solid company he built up over the years is in good hands and poised to continue for many years to come.

Bill is still quite young and will likely manage and run this business for many years. With regard to succession planning, it will then be Bill's turn to think about what will happen to the business once he is ready to retire or something happens to him. Bill is not married and currently doesn't have any children, so he will have to think carefully about the future plans for the business.

In this case, the smooth transition from one generation to the next was possible because both father and son were open to, and agreed to, the plan of action. And it was great that when the ownership and leadership changed hands, there was barely a blip in the business. Over the years, Bill's father groomed him to be the natural successor in this business, so the successful transition came after years of preparation. Had Bill not been actively involved and passionate about the business, he may not have been able or ready to receive the baton when his dad handed it over to him.

An Alternative Transition Plan

Dr. M is a successful chiropractor who owns his practice as a sole proprietorship with a cost-sharing partnership in place. Over the years, his practice has steadily grown and Dr. M helps many patients maintain and enhance their health by providing outstanding service. Dr. M's business relies on him to be there because he provides the service and care his patients need. He has built a name for himself and his patients continue to come to him because of his excellent reputation and the service he provides.

Dr. M is in his early thirties, is married, and doesn't yet have any children. His wife is a teacher. He and his wife have a solid investment portfolio that provides long-term growth and a bit of cash flow. Dr. M sees the value in having multiple streams of income, and for him, getting some of their money to work for them is important in supplementing the income they work hard to earn.

Even though he is quite young, Dr. M has spent a lot of time thinking about and planning for his eventual transition out of his business. Unlike Bill in the previous story, Dr. M's business will not likely pass on within the family but will rather be sold to a third party. Dr. M already has a mechanism in place so that the individual with whom he has the cost-sharing arrangement has the first right of refusal to buy his practice should anything happen to him.

However, Dr. M is thinking ahead and is actively working to grow and maximize the value of his practice so that should he decide to sell, it will be appealing to many potential buyers. Not only does he work "in" the business but he spends a significant amount of time working "on" the business and this includes succession planning. He is already putting strategies in place so that he can exit his practice smoothly when the time is right. And if anything happens to him, his business is in a position to be sold, which will make things easier for his wife.

A Bumpy Ride

This last story I share is from a case study I worked on during an executive training program I attended. It is an example of what happens when there is no properly documented plan in place.

We'll call this entrepreneur Mr. X. Mr. X was a highly successful businessman who founded, owned, and operated a successful service company. He loved his business, spent years building it up, and was a solid leader and visionary. His efforts kept his company growing and moving forward year after year. He had a small staff and they were spread out across the country. Some lived in the same area as Mr. X but he didn't feel he needed a physical office space. He allowed his staff to work from home, which in his mind was a win-win because it gave them flexibility and it saved on overhead.

All was well until one day Mr. X suffered a severe stroke. In the blink of an eye, he was out of the picture and unable to oversee his business. His wife (who was not actively involved in the business) was suddenly left holding the bag. Mr. X didn't have any business partners nor did he have anyone he was grooming to take over his leadership position. So, his wife grabbed the reins and tried to oversee a business that she didn't really know anything about.

Mr. X survived the stroke, but his recovery was long and riddled with complications. Over time, without a leader and visionary, the business began to decline. No one was there to bring in sales. As sales began to fall and expenses continued to come in, Mrs. X did the only thing she could, she began letting go of some of the staff members.

Because the team didn't connect in person and were spread out across the country, they felt disjointed. Mr. X was the one who had kept it all together, and without him, there wasn't much of a team. Each of these staff members had specific roles within the organization, but none were really capable of rallying the troops and continuing to grow the business.

In a matter of months, the value of Mr. X's business dropped dramatically, and his business was at risk of completely falling apart.

Eventually, Mr. X recovered and came back to find that all of his hard work over the years was reduced to almost nothing. He had no one to blame but himself. When he was finally able to take over again, he basically had to start from scratch and rebuild everything, and he was fortunate that he was able to rebuild. But during the time that he had been ill, his wife, family, and staff members had struggled. I'm sure he never intended to burden them with such difficult issues, but by not planning ahead, he had allowed for such a situation to happen.

So, again, for those who don't think estate and succession planning is a priority, think again. When it suddenly becomes a priority, it's probably too late.

≡CHAPTER≡

Leave a Roadmap to Find the Treasure

Thinking about and working through your estate and succession planning takes dedicated time and effort, as well as collaboration with your team of professionals. But it's the best way to ensure that all of the fruits of your labor over the years are protected and eventually passed along in a manner that makes you happy. You'll probably end up with pages of notes with your personal thoughts, as well as notes from all of the meetings you have along the way with your estate planning advisor, lawyer, accountant, work team, and family members.

The last and most important step is to thoroughly *document* everything so your instructions are clear and easy to follow. Keep in mind that your estate plan is not a fixed document—I highly recommend reviewing and updating it on a regular basis. Various things in your life may change, and major life events may cause you to rethink how you want things done, so keep your documents up to date.

Below are some of the documents you will need to create. And then safely store them somewhere so they can't be tampered with.

Confidential Estate Planning Intake Form

Often when you work with an estate planning professional, they will ask you to begin by filling in a confidential estate planning *intake* form. This form is used to gather as much information as possible on everything contained in your estate.

This is why I recommended earlier that you take the time to create your baseline and get a solid understanding of what you are working with. This intake form is just a brief summary, but it helps guide the conversation with your team and ensures that you cover all the necessary items.

After your estate planning consultant takes some time to review the intake form, the next step is usually a face-to-face meeting to go over things together and talk in more detail about the best way to proceed.

In the next chapter, I provide a checklist of the documents you should gather so you can fill out the intake form provided.

Overall Estate Plan

To be honest, some days I forget what I ate for breakfast even before lunch hour. In any case, when you are doing your estate planning, I recommend that during the process, you take detailed notes on what you and your team are putting into place. When you're working on something as important as your estate plan, you want to make sure you have carefully documented *everything*. Even though you think you'll remember, the truth is you won't.

After you meet with your team of professionals, I recommend drafting a written estate plan that you and your family can refer to and update as need be. This is a document separate from all the legal documents (will, power of attorney, etc.); it is an informal summary of your estate plan written out in your own words and therefore simple to understand. A lot can get lost in translation when it comes to the formality of legal mumbo jumbo so make your own set of easily understandable cheat sheets. Think of it like a business plan outlining the details of your estate or a personal collection of thoughts and notes that outline your intentions.

This can be as simple as having a dedicated notebook where you keep all your thoughts and meeting notes. Or perhaps you can put together a binder containing your thoughts, notes, and any articles or information you have gathered during the process.

I use a plastic file bin to keep all my articles, notes, and important documents pertaining to our family estate and succession planning information. It's a bin that is separate from all our other household files. I've created tabs for the different things that are covered, and these include:

Reference Documents (estate and succession planning articles and research)

- Meeting Notes
- Legal
- Accounting
- Financial Planning
- Financial Documents
- Insurance Documents

Each of these sections contains multiple files. For instance, my "Meeting Notes" section contains files labelled with the date of each meeting.

In the bin, which is stored in our den, I keep all of the rough notes, information sheets, and other documents we receive from our team of experts, as well as anything related to estate and succession planning.

The point is to find a method of documenting the process and storing everything so you can find things easily and refer back to your notes as needed.

Business Succession Plan

When you have a business, it is essential to have a written succession plan supported by all the legal documents needed to enforce your wishes. Again, your team of professionals will create formal legal documents, but just as with the overall estate plan, I believe you should have an informal document you can refer to and update along the way.

Your business succession plan should address questions such as:

1. What happens to ownership (or your share of the business) if you die? For instance, if you have a business partner, do they get first dibs at purchasing your shares? Do they need to approve whomever you decide to leave your shares to? These are important things to be discussed and documented early on.

2. In the event that you become incapacitated and unable to run the business, is there someone in place who can oversee it and ensure that operations continue smoothly? If not, is this something you are looking to address in the near future?

3. If you become ill, unable to communicate, or incapacitated for a period of time, who will have authorization to deal with your busi-

ness bank accounts, investment accounts, etc.? Also, who will have authority to make financial decisions in your absence?

4. What are your long-term plans for your business? Are the actions you are taking today bringing you closer to achieving these goals?

5. If you plan to pass the business on to family members, are you sure they are on board for this responsibility? And do they have the skills and qualifications to take over your business?

Your Last Will and Testament, a Living Trust, or Both?

As I mentioned earlier, I'm no expert at how to best structure things. My goal is to get you thinking about a plan that will best meet your wishes by considering the impact and legacy you want to leave behind.

The "how-to" will be outlined by your team of experts. Some people simply have a will, while others have more complex structures, such as a living trust. A living trust is similar to a will in that it is a trust created while you are alive, and it outlines your wishes regarding your assets, dependents, and heirs. The main difference is that a will only becomes effective after you die and it enters into probate. A living trust, on the other hand, can bypass the lengthy probate process, allowing your trustee to carry out your wishes. Your team of experts can explain the pros and cons in more detail and recommend the path to follow, based on your individual circumstances.

Your lawyer will take all of the instructions and information you provide and prepare your formal documents—which will be referred to in the event that anything happens to you. My lawyer's office holds a copy of my current will, and they have provided me with a binder that summarizes everything. Included in the package that they gave me are several business cards for my lawyer's law firm. My family knows that if anything happens to me, the first thing they need to do is get in touch with my lawyer.

Within my will, I appointed an executor who will work with my lawyer to ensure all of the instructions in my will are carried out.

Insurance Documents

Keep your life insurance documents in a place that is safe and also accessible to your family. Your family should know which insurance company you use so they can contact the firm when the time comes. You don't have to share all the details of your policy, but by giving them the contact information for your insurance agent, they will at least know a policy is in place.

Sadly, sometimes people don't know whether or not their loved ones have policies in place, and as such they never follow up to submit a claim. Don't let this happen to your family. Make sure to let your family know that a policy exists and include the details of your insurance information in your will.

It's usually up to the beneficiaries to notify an insurance company and submit a claim when someone dies. But they can't do that if you haven't told them what policies you have in place. You may have paid hundreds of thousands of dollars in insurance premiums for the sole purpose of protecting your family, only for the money to go unclaimed if your family members aren't aware of their existence. They may not even bother looking if they assume that you surely would have told them if you had such a thing. Unless an investigation is done, or for some reason they decide to start inquiring about what insurance you had, they may never receive what you intended to leave for them.

List of Assets, Financial and Investment Accounts, etc.

In an earlier chapter, we worked through creating a baseline that outlines your estate as it looks today. Leaving a copy of this summary with your will makes it easier for your lawyer and executor to move things forward, and it will make things less stressful for your family. Of course, it's important that you have kept your summary up to date over the years.

Preplanned Funeral and Burial Paperwork

As discussed earlier, preplanning and paying for your funeral service and burial is quite common. By doing so, you are able to convey exactly how you want things to be done. This takes away any conflict that may arise between family members regarding your wishes. No need to argue about whether or not you wish to be cremated, or which casket you would prefer, or what flowers you like best.

When you pass, it will likely be a sad and difficult time for your family.

They will be in mourning and having to make funeral and burial decisions would be an added stressor. By taking care of things in advance, you save them the trouble and the financial burden of having to do this at a time when they are struggling with your loss.

Make sure to keep a copy of your preplanned funeral and burial or cremation paperwork with your estate planning documents. If your family knows that you have already done this, it will ease the burden they have to deal with upon your death.

Contact Information for Your Estate Planning Advisor or Lawyer

At a minimum, be sure that your family has the name and contact information of your estate planning advisor and/or lawyer. Keep this information with your important family documents and perhaps keep a business card in your files. Let them know that if anything happens to *you*, their first step should be to contact your advisor for detailed instructions.

Appointing an Executor

Selecting an executor for your estate shouldn't be taken lightly. Being an executor is a challenging, emotional, and overwhelming task that requires patience, organization, good communication, and good project management skills. Think about it: you've likely been on this earth for decades, and now someone has to take care of wrapping up all your affairs. Not an easy or desirable task.

This is an important role, and when selecting an individual for this, you should be confident that they will understand and be able to oversee the entire process properly. Select someone whom you trust and whom you feel would be strong and capable enough to fulfill all the duties of an executor.

I suggest leaving a checklist of executor duties with your estate planning documentation. This will be helpful for your executor when the time comes, and they can use the checklist to make sure they stay on track. In addition, if you take the time to understand the role of the executor, you can make an effort to organize your affairs so the information and documentation they need to fulfill their duties will be easily accessible.

The Duties of an Executor

Most definitions of an executor are simplified and often don't convey the amount of time and effort that goes into fulfilling the duties that are involved. In Chapter 11 – Resource Guide, you will find a useful checklist that outlines the duties of an executor.

Review and Update Regularly

The last thing to keep in mind is that life is not static; your life circumstances will typically change for various reasons. The value of your estate will fluctuate over time, but if you acquire any major assets, it would be important to update your documents to include these acquisitions.

You may also go through changes with your family situation, so be sure to make updates to reflect the changes. Can you imagine going through a nasty divorce, rebuilding your life with a new relationship, new family, new business, or whatever else you may acquire—and then neglecting to update your documents?! How would your family feel if something happened to you and your entire estate went to your ex-spouse because you forgot to update your files? Not a pleasant thought, is it? So, remember to review regularly and update as needed.

Final Thoughts

Estate and succession planning shouldn't be viewed as a chore or annoying task that just needs to be done. It should be viewed as one of the greatest acts of love toward your family and loved ones. Ask yourself the question, "Do I care what happens to my family and/or loved ones after I'm gone?" For the majority of people, I believe the answer would be yes. Which begs the question: why haven't more people done their estate and succession planning?

It is said that *actions* speak louder than words, so show them that you care by getting your affairs in order. I regularly work on keeping my estate and succession planning in order so that when my time comes, my family can celebrate my life and not be stressed out by my death. It won't take away the sadness or grief, but it will allow my family to reap the rewards of all I have built up over my lifetime. And hopefully they will follow in my footsteps and be able to pass the wealth along for generations to come.

≡CHAPTER≡

A Useful Guide to Resources and Examples

To help you get started, I've included some resources that you might find useful and that can serve as a foundation for you to begin putting your plans together. Keep in mind that legislation, regulations, and rules sometimes change, so keep your eyes open for updated information.

I wrote this book to emphasize the importance and the "Why" of estate and succession planning. I also wanted to make sure I addressed the emotional side of the topic, so many of the resources that I provide address this aspect. Remember that this book isn't meant to be an overall "how to" regarding the business of estate planning, as there are numerous other resources out there that cover those aspects. In addition, your experienced team will be guiding you through the "how tos" when the time comes. Meanwhile, you need to focus on taking action towards putting your plan in place, a plan that will most benefit the members of your family and that will help them to avoid any possible uncertainties or conflicts.

Suggested Books
- *Every Family's Business* by Tom Deans
- *Willing Wisdom* by Tom Deans
- *Built to Sell* by John Warrillow
- *They Left Us Everything* by Plum Johnson
- *Perpetuating the Family Business* by John L. Ward

Online Resources
All you need to do is Google "estate and succession planning" and you will find that there is a flood of information available online. I'm not going to list specific sites, as each year things change and new information

becomes available, so take the time to do an up-to-date search and look through the sites to see which ones will work best for you. Be careful not to let yourself get overwhelmed by the volume of information. I suggest reading through articles that may be relevant to your situation and taking some basic notes. Don't get too caught up in the minor details, as each family's situation is unique.

Use the internet to identify and research potential advisors that can help you on your journey, or you may have friends who have worked with advisors that they highly recommend. As mentioned, I suggest finding an experienced and reputable estate and succession planning consultant who can walk you through the process and guide you step by step. Take the time to read the reviews for these consultants or experts and find out how others have rated their experience with each consultant or firm. It's important to find someone you feel comfortable working with, so don't just jump at the first name that pops up. Do your research and once you've narrowed your list down, interview each person to determine whom you would like to work with.

In addition to finding general information on estate and succession planning, you can also do some basic research that is specific to your country and province or state. Tax and estate laws vary, and hopefully the team you put in place will be able to explain what these laws mean for you. But if you want to get a head start, you can always do some reading online, which will allow you to ask specific questions.

Look Within Your Existing Network

A great way to get started is to talk to some of the professionals with whom you already have relationships. Your accountant, lawyer, financial planner, or banker will likely be able to refer you to reputable and experienced estate planning specialists. Or, you may have family, friends, peers, or associates who have gone through the process already and may be able to share their experience and whom they have worked with. Ask around, get feedback, and take a look at reviews for some of the recommended specialists. Then once you have narrowed down your list, you can begin setting up some initial consultations to determine whom you are most comfortable working with.

Other Resources

Getting started can be overwhelming, so I am including a few tools that you may find helpful as you begin your estate planning journey.

ESTATE PLANNING CHECKLIST – ITEMS TO GATHER BEFORE GETTING STARTED

Of course, you will need only some of them, depending on your circumstances.

Current Estate Planning Documents
- Current will (if you have one)
- Powers of Attorney for property
- Powers of Attorney for personal care
- Powers of Attorney for business

Marriage, Separation, Divorce Paperwork
- Marriage Certificate
- Marriage Contract
- Cohabitation Agreement
- Separation Agreement
- Divorce Paperwork
- Court Orders

Property
- Summary/list of all properties owned
- Joint venture agreements (if owned jointly)
- Property deeds
- Current mortgage statements

Financial
- Net worth statement (see sample template)

Banking
- Most recent bank account statements for all accounts

Investments

- Most recent statements for nonregistered investments
- Most recent statements for registered investments
- Proof of beneficiary designation for each plan

Business

- Copy of current succession plan (if you have one)
- Partnership Agreements
- Shareholders Agreements
- Buy/Sell Agreements
- Corporation paperwork and minute books
- Diagram outlining interconnection between businesses (if any)

Insurance

- Life Insurance policies (make sure to gather all policies—personal, through company benefit plan, any life insurance policies on mortgages, etc.)
- Proof of Beneficiary designation for each policy

Registered Pension Plan

- Most recent statement

Income Tax Returns

- Most recent tax return and notice of assessment

NET WORTH STATEMENT				
Net worth (as at _____)				
Assets		**Liabilities**		
Principal Residence		Mortgage		
Vacation Home/Secondary Residence		Mortgage		
Investment Property 1		Mortgage		
Investment Property 2		Mortgage		
Investment Property 3		Mortgage		
Investment Property 4		Mortgage		
Chequing account 1		Loans, etc.	Current Bal	Limit
Chequing account 1		Line of credit		
Savings account 1		Line of credit		

NET WORTH STATEMENT (CONT'D)					
GICs		Loan			
Non-registered investment Account		Loan			
Registered investment Account					
Ethan's bank account					
		Credit Cards	Current Bal	Limit	
Vehicles		VISA			
Jewelry		Mastercard			
Art		American Express			
Other Assets		Other			
Total Assets		Total Liabilities	$		
		Net worth	$		

QUESTIONS TO THINK ABOUT BEFORE GETTING STARTED

- Who do you want to include or who should be involved in your estate planning process?
- Who will be the executor of your will?
- Who will be the beneficiaries of your insurance policies, your will, etc.?
- Do you plan to leave a portion of your estate to a charitable organization?
- Do you have adequate life insurance or financial resources to support your family if you are the primary breadwinner and something happens to you?
- What are your wishes with regards to guardianship of your children?
- What are your wishes for your pets?
- Who do you think should have Power of Attorney over your affairs if something happens to you and you are not capable of making decisions or taking action?
- What do you want to happen if you become gravely ill, injured, or unable to direct medical professionals with regard to your care? Who will be authorized to make decisions for your care if you can't?

- Are you an organ donor? If so, is your family aware of this decision? If not, will you talk to them about this so it doesn't come up as a surprise if anything happens to you?
- What type of funeral service and arrangements would you like? Do you want to be buried or cremated? Would you like to preplan these things and prepay for them?
- If you have a business, is there a business continuity plan in place should anything happen to you? What would be the impact on your business if you were suddenly unable to be involved in operations?
- If something were to happen to you, would your family want to take over your business or would they likely have to sell it?

DUTIES OF AN EXECUTOR

The role of an executor can be emotional and challenging. When you select an executor, make sure you pick someone who will be diligent and accountable with your affairs. Also, be sure to pick someone whom you think can handle the stresses and challenges of the job. Being an executor can be a burdensome job and selecting the right person for this shouldn't be taken lightly.

An executor is responsible for identifying and gathering the estate assets, paying off all debts, and then dividing the rest among the beneficiaries. An executor will work to ensure that what you have outlined in your will is rolled out according to plan.

Below is a list, put together by blogger Jim Yih, of some of the key executor's duties. Keep this list in mind when thinking about who you want to appoint as your executor.

1. Immediately After Death
- Arrange for organ donation, if applicable.
- Arrange for funeral.
- Need the proof of death (from the funeral home).
- Need to apply for a Death Certificate (from the government).
- Review will with lawyer.
- Arrange for care of dependents and pets, if applicable.

- Find and secure all assets: home, contents of home, other real estate, personal property, business, vehicle, perishable goods, safety deposit box.
- Obtain insurance for any vacant real estate.

2. Very Soon After Death

- Pay for funeral.
- Find all ongoing expenses and debts.
- Stop all unnecessary expenses: subscriptions (magazine, theatre), healthcare (home care), memberships (gym, club, sports, auto, professional, etc.), entertainment (cable, satellite, websites), communication (telephone, cell phone, internet), insurance (auto, disability).
- Cancel Social Insurance Number, passport, drivers licence, and health card (to avoid identity theft).
- Forward mail.
- Notify all holders of assets: bank, broker, investment advisor, insurer.
- Notify all service providers: utility companies, landlord, property maintenance.
- Notify Service Canada regarding CPP survivor's benefit, Old Age Security, and Guaranteed Income Supplement.
- Cancel credit and debit cards.
- Review all documents relating to assets: property insurance, mortgage, lease, business, investment.
- Review all documents relating to financial obligations: contracts, divorce or separation agreement, court orders.

3. Soon After Death

- Establish an estate bank account.
- Arrange a meeting with an investment advisor.
- Institute a plan for securing and managing assets until sale, disposal or distribution.
- Reregister or transfer ownership of all assets to the estate.
- Obtain valuation of all assets.
- Prepare inventory of assets and liabilities.
- Schedule payment of all debts.

- Apply for probate of certificate of appointment.

4. Within Weeks of Death

- Meet with all beneficiaries of the estate.
- Maintain or initiate legal actions on behalf of the estate.
- Defend legal actions against the estate.
- Advertise for creditors.
- Collect life insurance death benefits.
- Arrange for transfer of assets passing outside the estate: registered investments, jointly held accounts, and land.

5. Remaining Estate Settlement Process

- Maintain records of assets and estate administration.
- Sell assets, as appropriate.
- Collect debts.
- Pay debts.
- Litigate or settle all claims by or against the estate.
- File outstanding tax returns (including terminal return).
- File final estate tax returns.
- Obtain tax clearance certificate.
- Obtain interpretation of will.
- Distribute assets according to the will: to individuals, to charities, to trusts.
- Claim executor's fees.
- Obtain releases from beneficiaries.

Did you enjoy this book? Do you want to share it with members of a group, association, or company? Discounts are available on Legacy: A Guide to Successfully Transferring Wealth From One Generation to the Next when purchased in bulk! Contact Darkwood Publishing to get our discount schedule.

www.darkwoodpublishing.com
Email: info@darkwoodpublishing.com

Acknowledgements

I'd like to thank the Book Launchers team for helping me turn my thoughts into an amazing book. Thanks to Julie Broad for helping me nail down a great topic. Thanks to my writing coach, Tim Testa for tirelessly working with me to get everything out of my head and onto paper. Thanks to the content, copy editors and proof readers who made sure things were up to par. Thanks to Sarah Bean for helping me navigate the world of marketing. And thanks to Jacqueline Kyle for keeping me on track and encouraging me every step of the way.

Thank you to my peers, Grace Churchill, Matt Mandziuk, Dr. Matthew Russell, Elaine Geroche, Paolo Diaque, Blake Wyatt, William Hung, Laurence Mongeau who openly and authentically share their experiences and stories with me.

Thank you to those I look up to as mentors and role models, Tahani Aburaneh, Jacquie and Harvey Jaehn, Quentin D'Souza, Aaron Moore, Erwin Szeto, Brian Pulis, Monika and Vaughan Jazyk, Don Campbell, Russell Westcott, Sarah Makhomet, Oliver Manalese, Mike Gillespie, Alexis Dean, Kelsey Ramsden. You all lead by example and inspire me with your positive energy, attitudes and messages. You may not realize it but each of you has touched my life in some way and I have so much respect for each and every one of you.

Thank you to my family, friends, mentors, associates and support team members who always support, encourage and lift me up when I need it most. Peter and Nena Quinsay, Suzanne and Derrick Madriaga, Andrew Quinsay, Seema Patel, Tanya Despinic, Grace Marquez, Natalie Ribic, Kris and Charlene Mamaril, Kristian Mamaril, Mariejoy Minon and Alex Lim. I love you guys.

www.ingramcontent.com/pod-product-compliance
Lightning Source LLC
Chambersburg PA
CBHW030523210326
41597CB00013B/1012